ENCYCLOPEDIA OF
WHITE MAGIC

ENCYCLOPEDIA OF
WHITE
MAGIC

◆

A SEASONAL GUIDE

PADDY SLADE

HAMLYN

Editor Jane Lyle
Designer Bob Gordon
Main Illustration Sarah Govia
Production Controller Alyssum Ross
Commissioning Editor Linda Burroughs

This edition published in 1990 by the Hamlyn Publishing
Group Limited, a division of the Octopus Publishing
Group, Michelin House, 81 Fulham Road,
London SW3 6RB

ISBN 0 600 57141 6

Produced by Mandarin Offset – printed in Hong Kong.

CONTENTS

FOREWORD — 6

INTRODUCTION — 8

SAMHAINE — 24
31 OCTOBER

WINTER SOLSTICE — 38
21 or 22 DECEMBER

IMBOLC — 58
2 FEBRUARY

THE VERNAL EQUINOX — 70
21-22 MARCH

BELTAINE — 84
MAY EVE 30 APRIL

SUMMER SOLSTICE & MIDSUMMER DAY — 100
21 JUNE & 24 JUNE

LAMMAS – LUGHNASAD — 116
1-2 AUGUST

THE AUTUMNAL EQUINOX — 130
22-23 SEPTEMBER

MICHAELMAS — 142
29 SEPTEMBER

FULL CIRCLE — 154
31 OCTOBER

FOREWORD

WITH GENERAL INTEREST in the occult burgeoning in the last twenty years, it is small wonder that the book shops are overrun with information on every conceivable aspect of the subject. However, for every twenty books published only one will have the undeniable stamp of authority, which is why I am writing a foreword for this book and not the other nineteen!

About thirty books a month land on my desk for review and it is often a struggle to find something to say about them. Most are written by people who, unlike Paddy, appear to have had little in the way of serious magical training other than the reading of other people's books. It makes a great change when you find one that is written with humour, genuine knowledge, and a deep love of the subject itself, and, as a bonus, a bona fide 'village witch'. There are not many of them left.

Witchcraft has an incredibly ancient pedigree that reaches back into the early palaeolithic times. There are those who regard it merely as a remnant of the mystery religions that flourished in the golden age of the Mediterranean cultures, and it may well be that some aspects of these faiths gradually found their way into the practice of the Craft. Certainly much of the Greek herbal and healing law used in the temples of Aesculapius at Epidaurus can be discerned in the potions and practices of the witches. But in the main I think it must be acknowledged that the real basis of their religion stems from the early shamanic beliefs which are depicted with such strength and beauty in the cave paintings of Lascaux, Les Eyzies, and at Santander in northern Spain.

As Paddy herself says in her book, most people think of witches as being part of a coven or group of thirteen, but this is a fairly late idea that began about the early sixteen hundreds. For the most part witches worked alone because it was safer and because of the danger of travelling long distances—the next village could well be a day's or even two day's walk away. The larger the group, the more danger of betrayal. Certainly there were groups, indeed some whole villages were of the craft, including the local squire and the priest, but they were the exception rather than the rule.

Within the pages of this book you will find genuine practices, rituals, spells, chants, and information that have come down, mouth to ear in the traditional way. There are different kinds of witch: the Traditional, and such a one is the author of this book, and there are the Family witches where the practice is kept within blood members of one or at the most two families within a certain radius. These are the oldest and purest forms, but there are also the more modern practitioners such as the Alexandrian and the Gardnerian.

From earliest times up to the late thirteenth century witchcraft was still practised at one level or another in almost every village in England. After that time it went underground but it left behind a plethora of old folkways that even now persist, and keep our heritage alive: The 'Obby Oss' of Padstow, The Verderers Dance with the participants dressed in forest green and bearing antlers, The Old Tup ceremonies where a Ram is dressed up and made 'king' of the festivities; The Maypole and the Floral Dance, the more sinister Sword Dancers and their 'Teasers' and many, many, more.

In reading this book you will be awakening race memories of Merrie England, one that has almost passed away, for it is nothing more nor less than the Diary of a Country Witch. It will take you through an entire year of deceptively simple Craft workings, teach you the working spells that your ancestors knew and probably used themselves. A village witch did not simply work magic, she healed, she advised, she dowsed for water and for lost articles, she was a midwife and a vet, a layer out of the dead, and a gatherer of herbs. She worked the weather, raised winds for the sailors and calmed them down again. She found wives for the men and husbands for the girls and above all she worshipped the great primeval Mother Goddess and arranged her life around those titanic inner tides of life and death over which SHE has always ruled.

For me, reading Paddy's book has been a comfort because it means that the old ways have not entirely vanished, that there are a few, a very few, village witches left out there. This is a distillation of old wisdom written from the heart, without pretence, without a need to 'get across a message', an offering of knowledge from the long ago, to the here and now. Because of my own connections I can vouch for the validity of what is written here. Practices differed from village to village but there was an underlying thread that bound the Craft together, not just throughout England but throughout Europe as well. A witch in Brittany worked in pretty much the same way as did the witch in Cornwall or Devon. Civilization has swept us along in its wake, but in the villages of England some things never change.

DOLORES ASHCROFT-NOWICKI.

INTRODUCTION

THIS BOOK IS ABOUT traditional, seasonal magic. Generations of country witches have celebrated the cycles of nature, working in the kind of way closest to the Earth and the monthly phases of the Moon. Seasonal magic is neither black nor white, although occasionally it might be pale grey. I think of myself as a green witch. I am not even really sure what black magic is, although I have a niggling suspicion that it owes much to the novelist Dennis Wheatley, to Aleister Crowley, magician and self-styled 'Great Beast', and even more to a perverted Christianity. Such common knowledge as there is about witchcraft seems to have been culled from reports of the infamous witch trials of the past and is based upon confessions dragged from poor, illiterate women, most of whom were not witches at all, but who confessed to almost anything dreamed up by their imaginative tormentors to relieve the agony inflicted upon their bodies and minds.

Sadly, the idea of black magic delights the more sensational sections of the media, despite the fact that it is a nonsense anyway. Magic is an electrical current, and is as good or bad as the person using it. Truthful explanations given in television and press interviews are generally ignored, but give the press a juicy sex scandal, especially one that can be linked, even remotely, with witches, and enormous publicity follows. Black magicians have nothing to do with witchcraft, but all to do with Satanism, which is anti-Christ. Genuine witches are followers of the Old Religion; we worship a Goddess, and our religion was practised on Earth from the time of earliest mankind, long before any of the more recent ones found it necessary to fill the world with evil and devils.

Nevertheless, these fallacious ideas are deeply entrenched. A typical reaction came from a critic of *Earth Magic*, a television programme in which I took part. 'Why', he asked, 'if they are so innocent, do they make a pact with the devil?'. The short answer is we don't – not in blood, urine, or any other unmentionable substance. The devil is anti-Christ, and witches believe in Jesus as a very great teacher. Since man was a gatherer of food, a scavenger of meat and a follower of herds, he has worshipped the Earth, who gave him all his sustenance; water, without which he could not live; and the Moon, which gave him light in darkness. Much later, he learned to worship fire and the Sun; this is when a lot of sacrifices began. The Goddess, who gives life, does not require life to be taken in Her worship.

WITCHCRAFT AS I SEE IT

One of the first things I would like to correct is the idea that the Anglo-Saxon word *wicca* means 'craft of the wise'. *Wicca* was the Anglo-Saxon word for a female witch and was a term of abuse. The Saxons, like most reformed rakes, were extremely pious and did not like the supernatural, although they were very superstitious. The word for craft of the wise was 'wisdom' and its practitioners were 'wizards'.

Another common misconception is that the coven (simply part of the Latin word meaning 'to gather') numbers 13, and pays homage to a goat, or rather, a male leader disguised as a goat. He is sometimes pictured as the rather nasty Goat of Mendes, who had something to do with the Templars. Our God is horned, certainly, but his horns are those of a stag

and signify strength. Covens or groups are led by women, not men, and most village witches work by themselves. It is difficult enough to collect a dozen people nowadays to do a rite, especially in mid-week when most sabbats fall; at a time of curfew, when one needed to cover miles across other people's land and could be prosecuted for doing so, it would have been nearly impossible. There is a saying, 'Thou canst not be a witch alone'. This, far from being a witch's saw, is, in fact, a saying of the church and was an excuse for arraigning all the members of a family for a single offence.

SEX AND NUDITY

Naked, or 'sky-clad' (dreadful term) witches are actually a very recent phenomenon, dating back no further than the 1950s. Gerald Gardner, who claimed to have revived British witchcraft, was a nudist and thought it would be fun to incorporate this into his rituals. However, no tribe, primitive or otherwise, goes to meet its God unclothed. Even if they only cover themselves with mud, paint, leaves, or flowers, they put on something special. It would have been highly dangerous for anyone to have been naked at any time in our history, and at one time, poor people had only one garment, into which they were sewn at the beginning of winter; it did not come off again until it dropped off a year or more later.

Initiation rites featuring sexual intercourse are not part of seasonal magic, although I am told that they happen in some of the Wicca groups. In any case, they should not be referred to as 'The Great Rite'. This was, and still is, part of a ritual which married the God to the Earth through the medium of the Goddess.

A young priest and priestess, who had both reached the same stage of knowledge and development, performed this act in deep reverence and in privacy. In very ancient times, when the Great Rite was done to ensure the Earth's fertility, a feast followed the ceremony. Part of the celebration of fertility sometimes included a general sexual free-for-all (as do many parties outside the craft), but this was not part of the rite. Sex has always been a part of magic, but it has a very special place and usually takes place between life partners. Initiation by sex causes imbalance. The more experienced partner takes on a dangerous karmic debt on behalf of the newly initiated.

As an hereditary witch, I do not initiate people; not because I cannot, but because I do not feel called upon to do so. Village witches do not have formally constituted covens, grades or hierachy; so there are no High Priests or High Priestesses, or third, second and first grades. My own group consists of some witches who have been through what I call the 'schools' – Gardnerian, Alexandrian and so on – some cabbalistic magicians and some pagans. We all work in harmony, teaching and learning from one another.

WORSHIPPING THE GODDESS

What exactly do witches worship? Ultimately, the Light Beyond the Light. Some say that this would have been beyond our forefathers' knowledge, but would it? Why did our ancestors, the Old Ones, break their backs building such magnificent magical sites as Silbury Hill, the great long barrows and the vast henges? They had reasons far beyond anything we know; or, perhaps, that we are just beginning to comprehend.

We worship the Goddess, who is the Earth. Earth is the only planet in our own Solar System capable of supporting carbon-based life. There might be many other such planets in the universe, but we do not know of them. It is, however, considered heretical to offer worship to Her – our home, our bounty and our defence. We do what we can to protect and cherish Her and do not destroy Her children.

Witches do not worship the Moon, but look to her as a visible symbol of the Triple Goddess. In the Moon we see the same phases as the day, the month, and the year, and the faces of the Goddess Herself. The new, waxing Moon symbolizes the Maiden, who is also springtime and the morning; with this aspect we work for growth.

The Mother aspect is shown at full Moon and corresponds to summer and midday. We, that is village witches, do not work on the full Moon. Like the high tide, the mood is slack, simply staying still. We might go out and do a rite for beauty, but that is all. Far too many battles have been fought on a full Moon, mental hospitals are troubled, and even television stations are troubled by lunatics.

Once the Moon begins to wane, she becomes the Crone, autumn and evening. Work is done to send away problems and to banish evil. Finally, the dark Moon stands for midnight and winter; at this time we look within ourselves, examining both our work of the past and our expectations for the future.

THE BOOK OF SHADOWS

There was once, and possibly there still is in some far flung eastern province, a Book of Shadows. This was all about interpreting the future from the shapes of shadows. The book so beloved of modern witches, copied out word for word, including spelling mistakes, by every new aspirant to the craft, and strangely known by this name, is not part of village witchcraft nor of seasonal magic. I do not have one and neither did the wise women of old. For the most part, they were illiterate, so no book would have been of use to them. They learned everything by rote. I do have several books in which I put my rites and reactions to them, meditations, pathworkings, and my own spells. But then, I am not illiterate. I do not give these books to other people, either to read or copy, for the very good reason that no-one can read my writing. When my sons were away at school they brought my letters home, for neither they nor their teachers could read them.

I tell everyone who comes to me to make a book of their own. Nothing should be written in it but work done by oneself. It is also important to realize that spells, unless they are very general, must be made and used for a specific purpose. Mine are tailor-made to fit a given need, and do not come from ancient tomes read by a guttering candle in a cobweb-hung attic. Once used, their efficacy is exhausted. It is simply no use being lazy and using a spell taken from someone else. Part of every healing rite, for example, uses the bricks and mortar of one's intentions to construct the words of the spell which will include all you mean to do.

WITCHCRAFT FOR BEGINNERS

Before you read about our festivals in detail, you should have some idea of basic witchcraft and circle working. When I began teaching the craft, my students naturally wanted to take part in rites and festivals, so I had to include some basic principles of temple etiquette. It is a good idea to know your left from your right, for instance, and how to pass a cup, plate, or bowl. Although each seasonal rite is different, the basics remain the same.

It is advisable to have a bath or shower before coming to a rite, and from this time you become your magical self. You should go to the lavatory before putting on your robe; wash your hands and other relevant parts, as you should not go into a rite with traces of urine or anything else about your person. The reason is simple; you can never be really certain how long a rite will last, and you cannot leave a circle once it is raised.

If the temple is a living room, it should not be treated as a party place beforehand. Come in quietly, greet others, do what is asked of you to get the room ready, and then sit quietly with your script. This should be taken home afterwards, for you might need to refer to it later when making notes.

When you are sent to prepare yourself, go quietly. This is not a time for making jokes; that comes later. As you remove your outer everyday

clothes, you should be taking time for contemplation, putting on your magical persona. This is a time for concentration on the work to come. When you come into the temple, a bowl of water is offered, sweetened with hyssop or rosemary, both powerful astringent herbs, symbolizing both your inner and outer cleanliness.

Some rites incorporate simple dancing: turning circles, or passing first left then right shoulders, symbolizing the turning of the Earth or the Sun, or the spirals of the universe. Some are used with a chant and stamping. I had never found any difficulty with this, but children are not taught country dancing at school today, and adults are rarely used to moving in a body. Three years in the Women's Royal Air Force taught me to do this correctly, but I was astounded at how much practice it took to do even the simplest movement. Self-consciousness should never be part of a magician.

Cakes and wine
Cakes and wine are passed round the circle in a particular way, which at first often causes hilarious confusion. The plate is passed to your left, it is taken and offered back to you, you take your cake, and it is passed on round the circle. I have watched amazed while the plate whizzes round the circle with no one getting a share, and some cakes ending up on the floor. This also needs practice, but it is worth it. The cup of wine should be received, raised, drunk from, and passed on, using both hands, one at the base and the other at the rim. We do not have a priestess taking the cup round; if this is necessary, it should be done by the Officer of the West whose element is water.

Magic in nature
Further study includes walking in the countryside and learning about trees and herbs. It is necessary to know which tree is which, not only from their leaves, but from their overall shape, so that they are recognizable in winter. A good knowledge of herbs and other plants is also important; how to tell barley from wheat, cow parsley from wild cecily, and which part of cuckoo pint may be touched with impunity. We need a knowledge of the clouds and what they foretell, so we study the sky by day. At night we try to learn the major constellations and other star clusters. I believe that a basic knowledge of astronomy is important to the study of astrology.

SPELL CASTING

Imagine, if you will, a small room, lit by the light of one candle, which stands in a beautiful blue bowl. The room is empty, but has been thoroughly cleaned, tidied, and prepared before the candle is lit. The candle represents the light of wisdom and no temple is consecrated without it; no rite can be performed unless the candle is alight.

The one performing the rite enters. (She has already bathed and washed her hair, paying special attention to her hands, feet, and private parts, and has fasted for six hours to put her in the right frame of mind.) She holds a sprig of rosemary, gathered with the left hand at the time of the new Moon. It is placed in a glass of red wine, which is surrounded by five candles – pink, red, blue, green, and yellow. The priestess walks round the room three times, deosil (sunwise), thinking of the work she has to do. She then sits, with legs and arms uncrossed, meditating upon the work to come. She lights the pink candle and says:

May the spirit of my wish burn bright.

She lights the green candle and says:

May my wish always have a firm foundation.

She lights the yellow candle and says:

May my wish always be inspired.

She lights the blue candle and says:

May my wish find its strength within its own element.

She lights the red candle and says:

May my wish always have power.

Then she says the following:

May my wish always be
Right for you and right for me.
May our love be strong and pure
May it grow and endure.
Bring the one who's right for me
That I may no longer be
Alone and lonely in this plight
Grant, I ask, this wish tonight.

The candles are left to burn down, and the wine is poured over the roots of the rosemary bush. This should be done when the sun is in Scorpio Cancer, or Pisces; these are the Water signs and water stands for emotion. This is a very old spell of unknown origin.

Group working

Saying the spell aloud, and repeating it many times is always a good way to make it clear in your own mind. When our group works together, we know only the basis of what we want to do. As we each speak across the circle or the pentacle, a phrase is unwittingly repeated by everyone. This phrase then becomes the chant which encapsulates the work. When we find this, we begin the walk round the circle, repeating the chant, until we all stop together and point upwards with our wands or knives, to send the thought on its way.

Timing

A fire spell is usually done on Tuesday, when the Sun is in Sagittarius, Leo or Aries. It is usually one for strength of purpose, and you would use red candles. Burn the spell afterwards, having written it down first.

If the spell is for communication or anything to do with examinations, you would do it on Wednesday, at the hour of Mercury (which you calculate using an ephemeris) when the Sun is in Libra, Aquarius, or Gemini. You would use yellow candles and some sort of mercurial incense, such as gum tragacanth, clove, cinnamon, verbena, lime flowers, or lemon peel. If you have a small phial of quicksilver about your person, so much the better; do not use a clinical thermometer.

Earth spells for stability, constancy, and anything to do with the hearth, you do to Venus on Friday, using green candles, when the Sun is in Virgo, Taurus, or Capricorn; bury this spell.

For limitations or definitions you work to Saturn on Saturday, using dark candles. These may be very dark purple, brown, or even black, so long as they are not made of pitch, and you do not try to burn them upside down.

A WITCH'S GARDEN

In times gone by, every village witch had a magical garden full of herbs and flowers. Some books and stories describe such gardens as dark, overgrown, and joyless. I have seen some of these, especially in the suburbs, full of old bicycles, hamburger cartons and excreta. Is the witch population of Britain larger than even we thought? Perhaps you should see mine. Everything shoots up with such exuberance that perhaps it could be termed overgrown. Sunflowers, jasmine, roses, melilot, raspberries, and apples run riot. It faces south-west, is at the top of a steep hill, and is beautifully sunny for most of the day. The back lawn has been shaped like the Goddess. All the plants which traditionally keep witches away flourish. My poor little monkshood gets smothered annually by soapwort and mint, and my angelica is ten feet high.

My sons, their wives, and my grandchildren play cricket and rounders there, and splash in the pool; we have a little spring and stream running through it. On warm summer evenings, we have supper in the garden and watch the hot air balloons drifting overhead. We perform rites with half the village watching, together with cows, sheep, horses, buzzards, housemartins, cats, and dogs.

Witches, I hope you are beginning to understand, do not corrupt innocents; nor do we seek converts. If people want to join us and they meet our somewhat exacting standards, we will teach them all we can, but we do not go out into the highways and byways to harry those whose beliefs are different from our own. There are those who, under the guise of witchcraft, do all these things. They may take, or cause others to take drugs. They may do all manner of objectionable things. They may trail a faint smell of sulphur about their persons, and they may be downright evil. They may be many things, but they are NOT witches. This book is all about what witchcraft really means: a celebration of life.

SAMHAINE

31 OCTOBER

SAMHAINE IS THE END of the witches' year, and also its beginning. We begin with an ending because we are working with the continuous tides of nature, and one thing leads to another. When the leaves begin to fall, we get ready for the start of the pagan year. We play the game of 'Catch the Leaf' which is not so easy as you may think. Just as you clutch one, it rises or swirls away; the heat of the hand creates a little thermal. As the trees begin to show their skeletons and the first frosts whiten the grass, the only green left is the holly, and the ivy clinging round the bare trunks. This is the time of Samhaine.

Another name for this time is the West Wind Sabbat, for at this season we celebrate the end of autumn and the western quarter of the circle.

Samhaine is a nature festival, one of the four most ancient fire festivals, the others being Imbolc or Oimelc, Beltaine or Mayday, and Lughnasad or Lammas. Solar rites, which fall upon the Equinoxes and Solstices, were a later imposition upon the original Old Religion. This was not arbitrary or violent, merely the expansion of a theme.

The times between these festivals are almost equal; there are six weeks from a solar to a nature rite, and seven from nature to solar, making four equal divisions of thirteen weeks in the year. These form the structure of our calendar. In the days before there was a written calendar, Samhaine would have come on the first hoar frost, or when the oak lost his leaves, Imbolc, now 2 February, with the thaw and perhaps the first snowdrops, Beltaine, when the hawthorn blossomed, and Lughnasad with the cutting of the first sheaf of corn.

THE MEANING OF SAMHAINE

The origins of this word are obscure. One possible explanation is that it stems from a Gaelic word, pronounced something like 'saven'. This was the time when surplus stock was killed, both to provide meat for the winter months, the blood being mixed with grain to make a kind of haggis, and to conserve dwindling supplies of fodder for the nucleus of the flock. Traditionally, the scent of such a copious amount of blood was thought to attract the spirits of the dead.

When the veil is thin

At Samhaine the veil between our world and the Otherworld is thinnest, and it is thought to be the best time to attract those who have gone before. I must emphasize that, to witches, these are the spirits of the long dead – the old masters and leaders of our race, racial archetypes, and the great ones who have served the land. We are not spiritualists and do not try to contact Aunt Annie or Uncle Fred to find where they left a will or hid the silver. We understand that there is someone, or something, far greater than ourselves who can help us in our quest for knowledge, light and truth.

I prefer the second explanation of Samhaine, which follows on from this. The Ancient Greeks spoke very highly of the priesthood of the Hypoboreans, whom they called Samethoi, followers of an ancient God of the Underworld whose name closely resembled Samethos. These priests were shamans, and their role was to enter the Realms of the Dead at the time of the first frosts to conduct the souls of those departed from this life during the year to their place of rest, and to bring back knowledge and enlightenment. Their training was long and arduous because the one thing you must not do in the land of mists is lose your nerve. The Samethoi were the priesthood of the inhabitants of Britain before the Celts arrived and should not be confused with Druids, who were Celtic priests.

Curiously, the old Julian date of this festival was 11 November; this date now signifies a more modern festival of remembrance involving sacrifice and bloodshed on a vast scale.

Bonfire night

Another echo can be found on 5 November, known throughout Britain as Guy Fawkes or Bonfire Night. It seems that people would not be cheated of their pagan festivals and obligingly moved the date slightly. They continued to celebrate Samhaine under the noses of Puritan and church alike, disguised as the commemorative burning of poor Guy Fawkes, who nearly managed to blow up parliament in 1605.

RITE OF SAMHAINE

This rite should begin at about 11.30 p.m., preferably outside so that we can have a good fire and fireworks. Everyone taking part is expected to bring along a couple of rockets and a few fireworks (not the noisy kind), as well as a bottle of full-bodied wine and some food for the feast afterwards. We also have sparklers and garden flares ready. Scripts should have been in everyone's hands at least a week beforehand, to allow study of parts. It is difficult to read by the light of a fire and a couple of flickering candles; indeed, the fire at the beginning of the rite is merely glowing charcoal. People should be warmly dressed in robes and cloaks, for late October is no time to be standing about half clad.

Finding a site requires staff work. We must liaise with the local farmer to agree a place where a safe fire can be built. It should not be too close to sheep or cattle, although sheep are fascinated by these odd humans, and horses always join in if they can. Nettles, thistles, and rabbit holes must be removed or filled in. A good organizer will have considered the possibility of heavy rain and made contingency plans for celebrating the rite indoors.

Indoor preparations

People are organized to move furniture, vacuum and dust the room, and find a secure place for dogs and children. I do not like having children at a Samhaine rite. There are others far more suitable – Beltaine, Lughnasad or either of the Solstices.

A very small fire is made in a cauldron; we use candles instead of flares and make absolutely sure we are using indoor sparklers. The results of using outdoor sparklers indoors are catastrophic. I cannot understand why anyone should associate witches with the smell of sulphur; it is most unhappy and offensive. We try to go about the room wafting perfumed clouds of frankincense, larch and sandalwood.

Goodbye to the Old Year

Indoors or outside, one person, dressed in black, stands by the fire. She represents the Hag or Crone, the aspect of the Goddess who is about to go down to the Otherworld for the winter, as all plants do. Everyone else files into the temple, with the exception of the two men who represent the Oak and Holly Lords, the two sides of our God.

The Oak, whose power ends with the year itself, when His sap ceases to rise and His leaves fall, accompanies the Lady to the Otherworld where they will rest until the spring. Herne, the Holly Lord, stands outside the circle watching the slow dance of meditation as they leave on their journey and we say goodbye to the old year.

New Year's Day

At midnight the second part of the rite begins. If we are outside, fresh dry wood is put upon the fire and rockets are let off; if we are indoors, we light sparklers. We greet Herne the Hunter and invite Him into the circle, dancing round Him waving our lighted sparklers. We ask Him to protect us throughout the winter months and He accepts the task in a fairly long speech.

We all listen carefully. When He has finished, we cheer, let off the remaining fireworks, and pass round the cup and the oat cakes. To end the rite, we thank the Old Ones for coming, and suggest that it is time for them to leave; we leave out something from our feast for them. This is the origin of leaving something for Santa Claus.

Once all the lights and the fire have been extinguished, we leave the circle and change out of our robes into ordinary clothes or fancy dress for the party. This is a very important part of any festival, and is often properly incorporated into it. The food needs to be plentiful, for we have danced and done a lot of thinking out in the cold air, which always works up an appetite. We play all the games associated with Hallowe'en: apple bobbing, apple snatch, and scooping coins out of flour with our teeth. As

most of the games are messy, it is a good idea for the fancy dress to be old. When we have tired of all this, we sit round until the small hours telling ghost stories, the weirder the better, until we are too scared to put the lights on. Since there has been so much publicity about the dangers of drinking and driving, we turn the temple/party room into a dormitory.

SAMHAINE SYMBOLS

Astrologically, Samhaine is located in the sign of Scorpio which rules the Eighth House of Death and Rebirth. It is ruled, nowadays, by Pluto, who was the God of the Underworld, the Roman equivalent to the Druids' Dis. Before Pluto was discovered in the 1930s, the governing planet was Saturn, whom a friend calls, 'the unforgiving loveliness of wisdom'. Throughout Scorpio we have to face the consequences of any actions taken during the year. Issues not faced annually at Samhaine may need to be faced at our ultimate death, when we might not be strong enough. Each individual needs to balance himself ready for the year to come. This is the forerunner of the New Year's resolution.

For those who use the Tarot, the appropriate card is number 13, Death, a card which can signify the end of one cycle and the beginning of another or dramatic change.

The Samhaine tree
At this time, the Moon is known as the Elder Tree Moon. The elder tree is the embodiment of the Crone or Hag, the third face of the Goddess. One should always be very polite to the elder and ask permission before taking from her. In spring, when I collect elderflowers for wine or potions, or in autumn, when I collect berries for Elder Rob, I always say 'Madam, may I take your flowers/berries for my use?'. Then I wait, and it often seems that the tree shows me which I may cut. I add the words 'We humans suffer from coughs and sore throats, which your fruits can soothe' when taking the berries. There is a recipe for Elder Rob on page 35. It works wonders, and is very soothing, especially with the addition of the optional rum. Every part of the elder is good for something, from cosmetics to dyes, but never try to burn it. T'awd Girl does not like it; many a fire has been caused when a householder with an open fire was silly enough to use it. Elder wood spits violently, and the burning sparks can travel a long way.

Samhaine herbs
Thyme, associated with departed souls, and rosemary for remembrance are both herbs linked with this time of year.

Belladonna, or deadly nightshade, is often thought to be a witch's herb. The dried leaves and flowers may be added to incense, for their fumes help to open up the psyche and facilitate astral projection. They should always be handled with care, as they are very poisonous. Deadly nightshade was an ingredient of 'flying ointment', which also included several other hallucinogenic substances. Centuries ago, witches rubbed this on their bodies and broomsticks to induce the sensation of flying. It seems a shame to explode old saws, but my broomstick has never budged, even though I leave it out in a full Moon to charge it up. It is very good for sweeping up leaves, though. I have never had the courage to try flying ointment; I have the feeling that it would cause a very nasty rash.

Lastly, the narrow-leaved rue, *Ruta graveolens,* the herb o' Grace o' Sundays, is associated with Samhaine. This pretty plant has round, blue-grey leaves and small yellow flowers, and has been described as smelling of musty churches or Gorgonzola cheese. Rue has an astringency which can cleanse the soul. It is, appropriately, a flower of repentance.

A RECIPE FOR ELDER ROB

Take a large basket of very ripe elderberries. Strip them from the twigs, place in a covered pan with no added water. Put this into the oven on a very low heat, and let them sweat for several hours, preferably overnight.

Next day, strain the juices carefully and mix with honey to taste. Warm the mixture until the honey has all melted. Do not boil, or you will destroy the goodness. If you like, a little rum or whisky can be added. Take two or three teaspoons neat, or one tablespoon in warm water to soothe a cold or sore throat.

A CHANT FOR SAMHAINE EVE

The Lord is Holly and is Oak
Two sides of one – so say our folk.
The Oak Lord goes, the Holly stays
To help us through the winter days.

A SAMHAINE SPELL FOR A BEREAVEMENT

The Yew is great in age and girth
A symbol of both death and birth.
Endings and beginnings it will spin
At Samhaine, when the veil is thin.

Three times round its girth we tread
Releasing mourners from their dread.
A knife to cut the spirit free
From bonds imposed by family.
A bow to make the spirit fly
To resurrection by and by.

A sprig for mourners all we take,
To give them peace for their own sake.

SAMHAINE SPELLS

To See Your Future Love:

THE APPLE PEEL SPELL

Carefully peel an apple, making sure that the peel remains in one long, thin strip. Throw it over your left shoulder, and if it lands in one piece it will reveal the initial of your true love.

AN OXFORDSHIRE CUSTOM

An old Oxfordshire custom demanded that an unmarried girl armed with a borrowed scythe climbed over the walls of the churchyard on Samhaine night. Once inside she was supposed to cut down any hempseed plants growing there, while peering into the shadows to see an image of her future husband.

TO DISCOVER YOUR SWEETHEART'S TRUE FEELINGS

Each of a couple throws a nut into the fire. If the nuts explode, there is great love between them, but if they merely whimper, love is dying. If one nut explodes while the other sizzles, you may draw your own conclusions.

THE OAK APPLE SPELL

To see how faithful your lover is, place two oak apples in a bowl of water. If they float together, rest assured that your loved one is faithful. If they float apart, it is time you looked for another.

A Divination Spell

This requires the blade-bone of a sheep which, of course, you will have about your person. Scrape all the meat carefully from the bone, using anything but metal, which ruins the spell. Two people are needed: one to hold the bone over the left shoulder, and one to look through the thinnest part of the broad end. If this person has 'the sight', she should be able to answer questions put by curious members of the group.

Footprints

This gruesome foretelling requires the ashes from a fire. Riddle the ashes as the fire goes out, then tip them on to the hearth and go to bed. If there is a footprint in the ash the following morning, the person whose shoe fits the ghostly print is not long for this world.

For A Lucky Year

Place the ash from the Samhaine fire inside your shoes, and you will have a lucky year. You will also have dusty feet, but perhaps that doesn't matter.

An Old Samhaine Custom

Let the house fires go out with the end of the old year, and light a new one from the special Samhaine fire before it goes out. This symbolizes a clearing out of old ideas and a taking in of new ones.

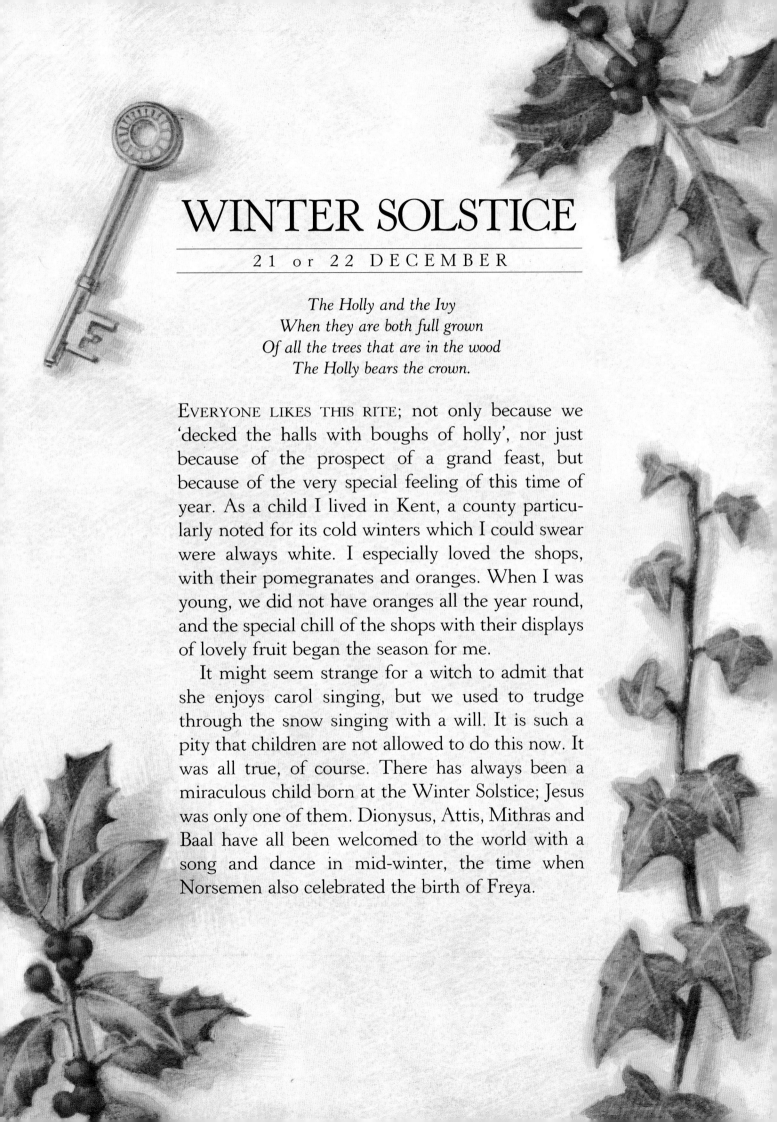

WINTER SOLSTICE

21 or 22 DECEMBER

The Holly and the Ivy
When they are both full grown
Of all the trees that are in the wood
The Holly bears the crown.

EVERYONE LIKES THIS RITE; not only because we 'decked the halls with boughs of holly', nor just because of the prospect of a grand feast, but because of the very special feeling of this time of year. As a child I lived in Kent, a county particularly noted for its cold winters which I could swear were always white. I especially loved the shops, with their pomegranates and oranges. When I was young, we did not have oranges all the year round, and the special chill of the shops with their displays of lovely fruit began the season for me.

It might seem strange for a witch to admit that she enjoys carol singing, but we used to trudge through the snow singing with a will. It is such a pity that children are not allowed to do this now. It was all true, of course. There has always been a miraculous child born at the Winter Solstice; Jesus was only one of them. Dionysus, Attis, Mithras and Baal have all been welcomed to the world with a song and dance in mid-winter, the time when Norsemen also celebrated the birth of Freya.

Witches do the same things as Christians do, but we did them first. We deck the house with as much greenery as we can, give presents and have a wonderful time. I have to prepare for at least three festivals: the Solstice, my annual party, and Christmas for my grandchildren. So I begin early, spending a lot of time making the food, including some extremely alcoholic trifles, which my mother called 'Tipsy Cake'.

Although we try to do a short rite out of doors, we have to do the main one inside, so I collect as much holly as I can beg from friends and acquaintances, enormous bundles of ivy, and slim, dead, ivy-covered trunks. I know a few places where mistletoe grows in abundance, and we also bring in some boughs of pine or larch.

Once everything is gathered in, I get my working party to clean the house. It is important to make sure that it is as clean as possible for all rites, since dirt can attract some curious elemental spirits. Then we begin decorating the room by stringing the ceiling and covering the lampshade with mistletoe. We thread ivy and tinsel round the strings and finally we put up the holly and some stars. Everyone wonders why we bothered to clean the floor. Any ivy-covered trunks are held in place against white sheets draped over bookcases, and we cover the walls with as much greenery as possible.

There is, of course, nowhere to sit; everyone is tired and we must have showers and get ready before the rest of the group, who begin to come early. We share a large bowl of steaming punch or a good thick soup. (We are not supposed to eat before a rite, but most people are hungry in winter.) Everyone goes upstairs to put on their best robes; a few, quick, magical passes and Abracadabra – the room is a temple, or rather, a snow-filled glade deep in a wood.

We have a priestess, a piper called Jack in the Green, a drummer, four quarter officers, and someone to work the tape recorder. This last is no easy task, for electrical equipment used in magical rites develops an unbelievable waywardness.

Incense and candles lit, wine and cakes ready, and we are set to begin my favourite rite of the year.

THE WINTER SOLSTICE RITE

The priestess is alone in the glade. She lights a very large, red candle, which stands in a cauldron surrounded by the best holly, ivy and mistletoe. When she feels that the atmosphere has stilled, she takes up a temple singing bowl, and runs a piece of mahogany rod around the edge. A strange belling noise reverberates through the glade. Jack in the Green and the drummer come in, sit down, and begin to play.

On hearing the music, the group approaches the door, where a door keeper, holding a bowl of hyssop-scented water and a clean towel, is standing. Each person rinses his or her hands before entering the glade. Once everyone is inside, they circle three times sunwise (deosil) round the glade to the music of pipe and drum, and then stand in an inward-facing circle.

Opening the Quarters

The four Officers take their places. Beginning in the east, and with all facing that way, they call up the Guardians, the Archetype and the Totem of each quarter in turn. We are all expected to visualize the same image. In the east we imagine an early morning in spring, Merlin the Archetype and the Totem Cernunnos, Stag of the Seven Tines. We should watch them approach through a misty woodland glade, alive with birdsong. Once the Officer of the East has this firmly in his mind, he lights a yellow candle and turns to the south. This is the signal for everyone to turn that way.

Here Arthur, King of Logres and Holder of the Sword of Albion, approaches the circle on a hot midday in high summer. Sometimes he is riding the Totem Epona, White Mare of the Sacred Hills. At other times she simply accompanies him. Epona lifts her beautiful white head, snuffles the air, and gallops towards the circle. A red candle is lit, and we turn to the west.

West, the place of water, has Morgan, Priestess of the Grail, as its Archetype. The Totem is Mona, Sacred Cow of the Western Isles who brings with her the sweet smell of hay. Everyone imagines a glowing autumn sunset over the sea, a blue candle is lit, and we turn to the north.

In the north we visualize Guinevere, Queen of the Round Table, and Artos, Great Bear of the North. These mythical figures are seen approaching through a frosty midnight landscape. A dark green candle is lit, and the circle is open.

When all is still once more, the priestess walks sunwise round the temple, holding a sword waist high straight out in front of her. She states the intent. Our piper begins playing a merry tune, while the drum beats out a ONE-two-three rhythm for the weaving dance. We pass alternate shoulders, touch hands, and – as my American friend puts it – make eye-contact. The dance winds down, and we sit thinking about the woods.

Our temple already resembles a snow-filled glade and further atmosphere is created by leaving the window open a fraction, so that we can hear the sound of wind in the trees. (On a still night we use a very good recording.) We are ready to visit the Sanctuary in the Woods.

Pathworking: The Sanctuary in the Woods

You are going to seek Herne who, at Samhaine, promised to protect you through the dark months of winter. To reach Him, you must make a journey through the year. You are seated; arise and go to your door. You know where the key is; unlock the door, step through into the rocky passage beyond, and look back at the door as you close it behind you. Remember, it is there for you at any time you feel afraid or worried during this journey.

Turn and look around you. It is a warm, early spring morning in a lovely wood. Snowdrops form a carpet beside a little river which runs chuckling over the stones beneath a narrow bridge. Silver birches and rowan trees are just coming into leaf, while the first new green shoots of honeysuckle and briar are unfolding. All around you is the sound of birdsong, and as you look along the stream you see a jewelled flash of colour; a kingfisher has come to bid you welcome.

Cross the bridge, and you will find a path. At each side are stones covered with lichens the colours of jade, coral and amber. Cushions of moss show brilliant green and soon you see primroses, smelling of warm honey, violets and wood anemones. To your left is a marshy place where willow shoots gleam golden in shafts of sunlight. An alder grows on firmer ground, still with its black cones from last year. Your path leads you through an orchard of old crab-apples with their pink and white blossom. Blackthorns are in bloom too, for the brave blackthorn has blossom before leaves.

The morning progresses. Small oaks are in leaf, hawthorn boughs are laden with blossom and there is a foam of elderflowers. You hear small creatures scurrying about their business, but you cannot see them yet. Birdsong and the rustle of wings fill the air. Farther along you hear a hard, rapid tapping and look up to see a woodpecker finding grubs for its young. All this bustle only intensifies the stillness and peace that surrounds you.

A magnificent old oak, its new spring leaves tipped with scarlet, stands at the top of a bank. You feel that you must pay your respects to this ancient sentinel of the wood. Here, you feel protected from harm for the oak was called 'the Armour of the House of the Forest' by those who fled from persecution. Somewhere ahead you hear a clear, high piping – a liquid melody of incredible beauty. You know you must follow, but by now it is midday in high summer, and you are very thirsty.

A little way on there is the sound of falling water, and there it is, coming from a crack in a rock and falling into a round obsidian bowl. As it overflows, it begins a crystal-clear brook banked with cresses, mints, and bog myrtle. Look, there is a little frog sitting on a leaf. Beside the bowl is a small ledge where a fine silver cup stands. Above this is a sign 'Drink Well, Traveller, Quench your thirst'. You know the water is safe. After drinking, you splash your face and wrists with the overflowing water and cross the stream by some ancient stepping stones worn smooth by the feet of many travellers, so take care.

The sound of piping merges with the songs of thrush and blackbird. Scramble up the bank to an archway of thorns. Go through. Here, at high summer, you find yourself among the great armoured beeches. Look up through the most delicate tracery in nature and see the bright blue sky. There is a jay – blue and buff with striped wings – speeding about its affairs. It is said that our ancient oak forests were planted by the jay. Great hollies stand out dark green even now. You notice that many animals are visible and they are all going your way.

As the afternoon fades into evening the trees take on their glorious autumn colouring. A pair of ashes stand like pillars on either side of the path; as you pass between them the wood changes character again. The trees are closer together, the piping has stopped and stillness deepens. Sycamores have turned gold, and through the mist a gold and silver birch glows like a lantern.

A large white barn owl glides silently by, seeming to lead you on. A pair of stoats, their bright brown coats turning white and the black tips of their tails standing out (for the stoat is an ermine in winter), dance and play in front of you. They stand up on their tails to say 'Hurry up', their bright eyes seeming to laugh at your slowness. The wind gets up, and the leaves race by. You catch as many as you can, for every one caught is a happy month to come. The wind dies down, with the last of the leaves. Suddenly, the stillness is shattered by a bellow and the sound of clashing horns. The rut has begun and the stags are competing for leadership of the hinds.

In front of you is a solid-looking wall of bramble and hawthorn, covered in leaves of amazing jewel-like colours; a few berries are still there for the small creatures. All the animals make for a small hole at the base and you feel that you, too, can wriggle through. When you emerge on the other side, you find it is a dark, mid-winter night. Snow lies deep, hard, and crisp upon the ground. All about you are hollies and some unearthly light shows up the berries, glittering on the frosty snow. Yew trees make a hidden place, lit by a huge white Moon. And there, beside an ancient stone, stands the great Horned Lord.

His eyes are deep and mysterious, yet full of love and humour, His features are chiselled, and upon His brow are the magnificent antlers of a seven-tined stag. This is the Lord of the Wild Wood. His horns change, becoming the delicate sweep of the goat horns of Pan – friend and protector of all His small brethren. His horns change back to the antlers, for the Lords of the Wild Wood are one and they keep faith with their subjects. This is the Holly Lord, who will see us through the winter: Herne the Hunter.

He beckons you forward with a smile. You know that from this Being you can draw strength and love. Do you dare? You may offer your love to Him. The music of the wind dies down, and He begins to speak. (Here, a tape is switched on, and a deep voice speaks the words of Herne.)

As the words die away, you hear the piping once again, blending with the sound of the wind as it softly stirs the branches. You begin to feel drowsy . . . Suddenly, an owl hoots. You find yourself sitting beneath the sentinel oak. The owl hoots once more and flies away. In the moonlit wood you can smell the scents of larch and pine, chilled by frost. And looking back into the shadows of the deep wood, something with horns moves majestically away.

Soon you stand up. Before you is the passage through which you entered the wood. Go along it and there is your door. Open it and go through, lock it and put the key away until next time.

You have been given an aspect of the Horned Lord to think about. Try to keep what He has said in your heart, and to come to understand all that you have seen and heard. When you are ready, return – and remember, there is a blessing on those who serve.

Closing the rite

After the pathworking our piper plays a soft melody until everyone is back with us. All stand. There is a candle for everyone present on a small table within the circle, and some for those who could not be with us. The priestess takes up the large red candle from the cauldron and goes to the table. She beckons the Officer of the East, who goes and lights his candle from the one the priestess holds and then returns to his place. Each member of the circle comes and does the same thing. If there is someone they particularly wish to remember, they light a candle for him.

When the circle reforms, we do another weaving dance and sing *The Holly and the Ivy* – a very ancient pagan song. In time gone by, a carol was a song sung to a dance, or a dance danced to a song. Following the dance, a cup of mead and a dish of oatcakes is passed round the circle.

> *Hail to the returning Sun.*
> *We drink to the Old Gods,*
> *To the Holly, and the Oak, and The Lady.*
> *A Merry Yule to all.*

Then we turn to the north. The officers close their quarters, extinguishing the quarter candle as they do so. They offer many thanks to all who came to the rite. Finally the priestess closes the circle, saying: 'The rite is ended. There is a blessing on those who serve.' At this point, we all turn to the right, moving three times widdershins (the way the Earth turns, to the right or counterclockwise). When the Officer of the North reaches the door, it is opened for her by the doorkeeper. Everyone files out and goes upstairs to change their clothes and keep quiet, for the priestess still has things to do.

She places the cauldron on the hearth, removes the cup and the pentacle where the oatcakes stood, washes them and puts them away. All other candles are left burning, but she trims the wicks before leaving the temple.

THE WINTER SOLSTICE FEAST

By the time the priestess has left the temple the others have changed out of their robes and have their jobs to do. While the men replace the furniture, the women prepare the feast. Everyone begins to sing and stamp, for we have been travelling in the high realms and need to ground ourselves. For this reason the feast should be substantial and the wine flow freely.

One year I made a terrible mistake; I prepared a complete seven-course medieval banquet for 18. Everyone had changed into rather splendid costumes, while I became the kitchen drudge, feeling as though I had been put through a wringer. It seemed appropriate.

Our party games include all the traditional ones: musical chairs, pass the parcel, and some slightly risqué ones with an orange. As the candles begin to gutter and the fire dies down, we gather around and tell horrific ghost stories to each other.

WINTER SOLSTICE PLANTS AND TREES

The holly is a symbol of life. It is supposed to cure chilblains if those unpleasant things are thrashed with a holly twig. But there are less painful methods.

There is an old superstition which says that if you have ivy growing up your walls, you are supposed to be protected from witchcraft. I have some lovely specimens climbing my walls.

The golden bough
Mistletoe, the golden bough, is reputed to protect the house from thunder and lightning. I use it to keep my blood-pressure down.

Several years ago, just after my eldest son was married, I sent him out on the afternoon of the Solstice to fetch some mistletoe. It was growing very high up in a willow tree that grew aslant a deep river. There had been heavy rain, so the water was about 12 metres, say 40 feet deep. But Bob was a soldier and had overcome worse hazards. It was growing dusk by the time he climbed the willow which, as I said, was high. He picked the bunch, then climbed a little higher to get another. By this time it was

quite dark and the wind was getting up. My new daughter-in-law came panting back to the house – Bob was stuck up the tree. Another son had to fire a running line, attached to a cross-bow bolt, over a branch. We hauled up a stout rope, Bob grabbed it but came down straight like a plumbline and dangled over the river. Luckily, he timed his jump just right and landed on the bank. The moral of this story is: gather your greenery in daylight, or you may not live to tell the tale.

SOLSTICE SYMBOLS

The Winter Solstice falls right at the end of the sign Sagittarius, the Archer. This sign rules the Ninth House of the Zodiac, which governs philosophy, religion, higher knowledge and travel. Sagittarius is ruled appropriately, by Jupiter the Bringer of Jollity and planet of expansion. In the Major Arcana of the Tarot the card is number 14, Temperance, a card of moderation, balance, self-realization, and new horizons.

A SOLSTICE LEGEND

The Halcyon Days fall seven days before the Solstice and seven days after. They were named after Halcyone, the wife of King Ceyx of Trachis who was drowned at this time of year. Halcyone was so broken-hearted that she threw herself into the sea rather than live without her beloved. Touched by her devotion, the Gods turned husband and wife into kingfishers. In those days kingfishers were believed to nest on platforms of weeds which floated on calm seas. The Gods promised that whenever kingfishers were brooding, the seas would remain calm.

MEETING A FOX

In His speech, Herne tells of hearing His voice in the bark of a dog fox on a frosty night. It is thought to be very lucky to meet a single fox, but an unlucky omen to meet several.

A blessing Spell For Winter Solstice

We ask a blessing on this house,
This happy Eve of Solstice time.
We sing and dance and make carouse
To celebrate deep Winter's clime.

For Herne is here, and Mistletoe.
The Holly and its berries bloom.
We dance a carol, round we go
The Ivy winds about the room.

With wine and cake we make a toast,
And bring a blessing to our host.

Solstice Eve Chant

The geese fly high this Solstice morn,
The woods are bare, the snow is deep.
We wait for Herne to sound His horn
To wake His children up from sleep
To celebrate this happy night,
When Winter may be put to flight.

Winter Solstice Chant

Geese and standing stones and mist,
Baying hounds and hooting owl,
Sparkling stars, and snow is crisp
Herne is here. Bring forth the Bowl.

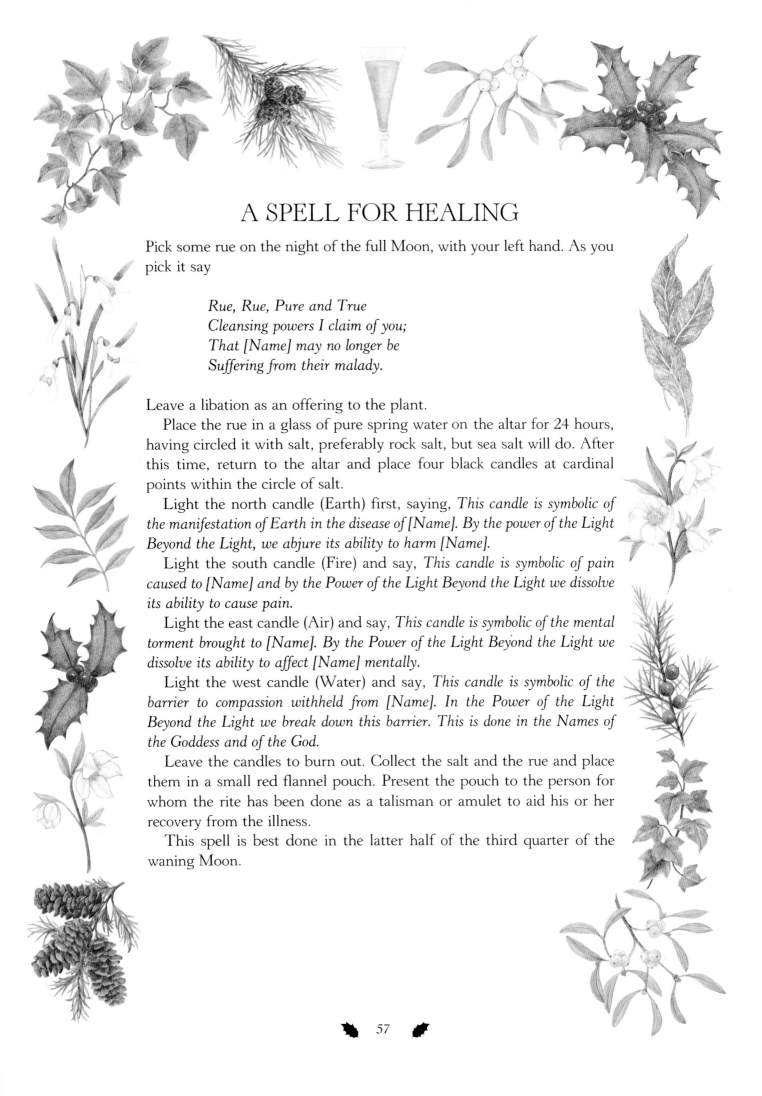

A SPELL FOR HEALING

Pick some rue on the night of the full Moon, with your left hand. As you pick it say

> *Rue, Rue, Pure and True*
> *Cleansing powers I claim of you;*
> *That [Name] may no longer be*
> *Suffering from their malady.*

Leave a libation as an offering to the plant.

Place the rue in a glass of pure spring water on the altar for 24 hours, having circled it with salt, preferably rock salt, but sea salt will do. After this time, return to the altar and place four black candles at cardinal points within the circle of salt.

Light the north candle (Earth) first, saying, *This candle is symbolic of the manifestation of Earth in the disease of [Name]. By the power of the Light Beyond the Light, we abjure its ability to harm [Name].*

Light the south candle (Fire) and say, *This candle is symbolic of pain caused to [Name] and by the Power of the Light Beyond the Light we dissolve its ability to cause pain.*

Light the east candle (Air) and say, *This candle is symbolic of the mental torment brought to [Name]. By the Power of the Light Beyond the Light we dissolve its ability to affect [Name] mentally.*

Light the west candle (Water) and say, *This candle is symbolic of the barrier to compassion withheld from [Name]. In the Power of the Light Beyond the Light we break down this barrier. This is done in the Names of the Goddess and of the God.*

Leave the candles to burn out. Collect the salt and the rue and place them in a small red flannel pouch. Present the pouch to the person for whom the rite has been done as a talisman or amulet to aid his or her recovery from the illness.

This spell is best done in the latter half of the third quarter of the waning Moon.

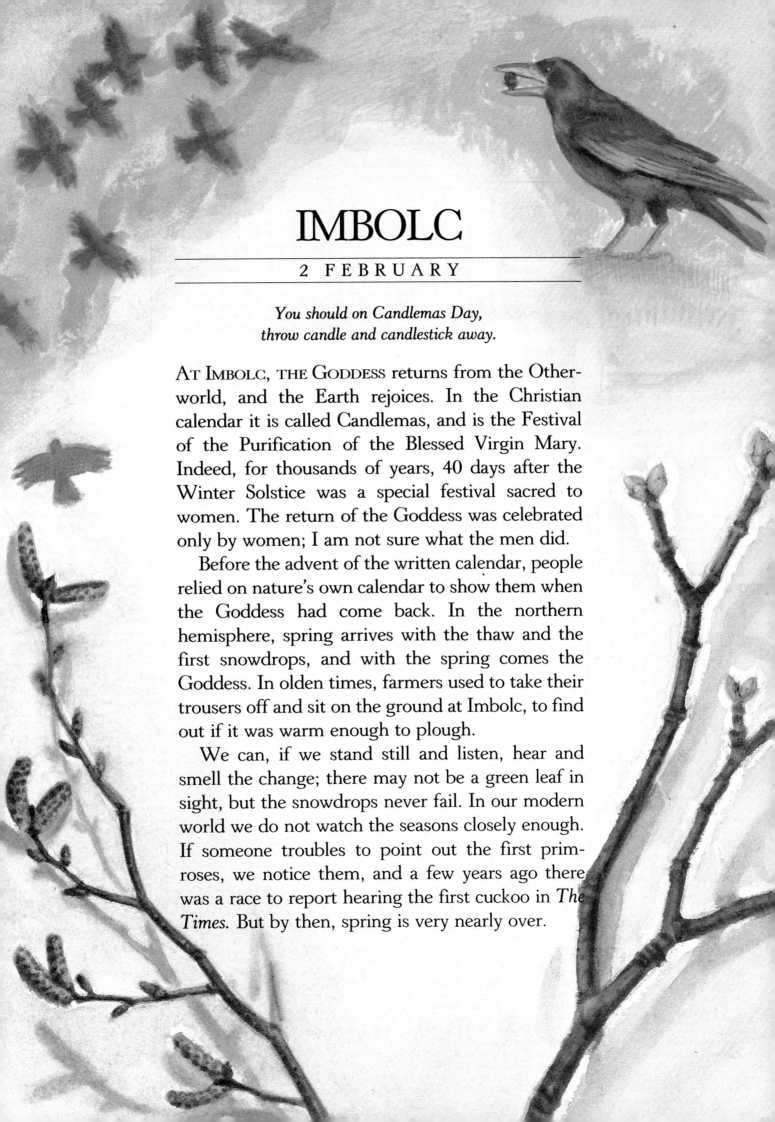

IMBOLC

2 FEBRUARY

You should on Candlemas Day,
throw candle and candlestick away.

AT IMBOLC, THE GODDESS returns from the Other-world, and the Earth rejoices. In the Christian calendar it is called Candlemas, and is the Festival of the Purification of the Blessed Virgin Mary. Indeed, for thousands of years, 40 days after the Winter Solstice was a special festival sacred to women. The return of the Goddess was celebrated only by women; I am not sure what the men did.

Before the advent of the written calendar, people relied on nature's own calendar to show them when the Goddess had come back. In the northern hemisphere, spring arrives with the thaw and the first snowdrops, and with the spring comes the Goddess. In olden times, farmers used to take their trousers off and sit on the ground at Imbolc, to find out if it was warm enough to plough.

We can, if we stand still and listen, hear and smell the change; there may not be a green leaf in sight, but the snowdrops never fail. In our modern world we do not watch the seasons closely enough. If someone troubles to point out the first prim-roses, we notice them, and a few years ago there was a race to report hearing the first cuckoo in *The Times*. But by then, spring is very nearly over.

In the olden days we did not pay much attention to the Sun, because we had a nature and not a solar religion. Today we do make much more of the fact that the days are getting longer, and the Sun grows stronger, if not much warmer. Winter is passing, and we make sure the Sun knows we are pleased. We give thanks that new life is all around us. Sounds of birdsong increase and the birds will soon be breeding; they are already repairing last year's nests, or making new ones. You can hear the young lambs in the fields, yelling for their mothers. (The old name for Imbolc was Oimelc, meaning ewe's milk.)

THE PREGNANT MAIDEN

Witches usually work on Imbolc Eve. It is quieter than other festivals, for we are, after all, welcoming the Maiden who is bearing the spring – conceived the previous Beltaine – within Her. It might be a little confusing to think of a pregnant Maiden. I can only say that She is rather like a heifer who remains a heifer until she has dropped her calf; but remember that the Maiden is forever virgin.

Imbolc is all about the re-awakening of the Earth after the long, dark winter months. It is about birth, and new beginnings. You could say that the Witches' Year begins again at every season, and that there is always something for which to give thanks.

ASPECTS OF THE GODDESS

A celebration suitable for a large group, who mostly stand in a circle watching the proceedings, involves three women, dressed in white, red, and black, to represent aspects of the Goddess. These three dance round the great Cauldron of Rebirth, chanting to the elementals of the four quarters:

> *Come to us from the Earth's four quarters*
> *Earth and Air and Fire and Water,*
> *Bring your minions to this home*
> *Sylphs, Undines, Salamanders, Gnomes.*
> *Ask your Captains, Nixsa, Djinn, Paralda, Ghob*
> *To bring them in.*

I cannot quote this rite at length, because it was written by Patricia Harrill-Morris, who kindly gave me permission to quote the above.

I should explain here that each of the quarters – Earth, Air, Fire and Water – has an elemental being. These are the Sylphs of the Air, Fiery Salamander, Undines of the Water Kingdom, and Gnomes, who belong to the Earth. Each element is also ruled by a King: Ghob for Earth, Paralda for Air, Djinn for Fire, and Nixsa for Water.

The full rite is quite long, involving a lot of dancing. Once, when taking part in this ritual, I grew very tired and out-of-breath. Our chant became so scrambled that it sounded as if I was saying Alexander's silk undies over and over again. Happily, I do not think anyone noticed. Keeping fit is a good idea, whether you are a witch or not; at least it ensures enough breath.

WHY IMBOLC IS WHITE

Each phase, or face of the Goddess has its own colour: white for the Maiden, red for the Mother, and black for the Crone. At Imbolc we use white flowers and candles to symbolize the Maiden. We make pretty chaplets of white flowers to place round the base of the candles. If we can find enough flowers we also make chaplets to wear.

AN IMBOLC RITE OF BLESSING FOR THE LAND

Some years we celebrate a rite of blessing for the land at this time. This involves stating our objectives, usually threefold: greeting the aspect of the Goddess then appearing in the sky, telling the Maiden of the Earth's need for Her return, and thanking Herne, the Holly Lord, for His protection.

We ask that, as the Moon changes her aspect and begins to wane, she takes the floods and rains away with her. In this way the land may dry out, and the crops can grow. The Moon governs the tides, and nearly all bodies of water; the waning Moon is traditionally the time for what are often called banishments, or getting rid of negative influences.

The entire rite is performed by five people. They stand in a pentacle, each at one of the five points, and each says a line of the rite. This helps create a good balance, something which is always important in magic. Between each part of the rite we hand round the cup of mead and the honey cakes.

Each person greets the Maiden, saying in turn:

1 *On this night we remember the Goddess who left us as Crone at Samhaine, and is to return to us. Come back to us, Lady, and bring the spring.*

2 *Lady, the snowdrops have pushed their way through the cold, wet earth, and we dream of your return. Come back to us, Lady, and bring the spring.*

3 *The birds return from their winter home. Come back to us, Lady, and bring the spring.*

4 *The plants which went down into earth with you are close to renewal. Come back to us, Lady, and bring the spring.*

5 *The trees are waiting to bring forth new leaves. Come back to us, Lady, and bring the spring.*

1 *Come back from the Caves of Annwn, where souls are purged of pain and sorrow.*

2 *Return from Hel, where souls are purged of grief and despair.*

3 *Come to us from the Mists of Avalon, from the Apple Orchard.*

4 *Come from Tir-nan-Og, the Land of Blessed Rest.*

5 *Return from the Land of Faerie, where you have dreamed long dreams of summer.*

THE IMBOLC TREE

Another name for this festival is the Ashgrove Esbat. The ash is one of the three most magical British trees, with oak and thorn. In Norse mythology the ash was the Yggdrasil – or World Tree – where the god Odin hung for nine days and nine nights before he was given knowledge of the runes, and then reborn.

Ash trees are mythologically the ancestors of mankind, and it is dangerous to destroy or cut one down. Ash wood does make a very useful quarter staff however. Ash trees protect us from lightning, can be used in divination and charms, and are often associated with Merlin. The ash traditionally protected folk from witchcraft: I have them all round my house, so I am well protected.

My grandfather had several split ash saplings. Passing a child who suffered from rickets or a rupture through the hole in the sapling was believed to cure him. These saplings were never cut down, because if they were, the disease would return.

IMBOLC BIRDS

The peacock, believed by many people to be very unlucky, is traditionally associated with Imbolc. It was bad luck to bring peacock feathers into the house because of the eye, which seems to stare out from each tail-feather. In England, a peacock's unearthly cry is said to foretell bad weather. But in India, it warns of tigers in the vicinity.

I would rather put the marsh tit in place of the peacock. Whenever we have a really cold February, this little bird visits my bird-table. I also love to watch the rooks at this time. It doesn't matter how many birds form the tumbling groups – they always sort themselves into pairs. They fly apart to do their acrobatics, but each returns to his mate between stunts. The old superstition that if rooks build high, it foretells a good summer is nonsense. In some of the wettest summers, rooks have built exceptionally high. In fact, they merely repair the nests of previous years.

IMBOLC SYMBOLS

Astrologically, Imbolc falls under the dominion of both Saturn and Uranus – co-rulers of the sign of Aquarius, and the Eleventh House. This House governs social matters, friendships, group relationships, hopes and wishes, and aspects of magic. Saturn is the planet of self-discipline, hard work and patience; Uranus, the planet of dramatic change, invention, and freedom. The colour allocated to Aquarius, The Water Bearer, is amethyst, or violet. Since one of the earliest spring flowers is the violet, this is quite appropriate.

The Tarot card here is number 17, the Star, which symbolizes hope and bright prospects for the future.

TWO THRESHOLD BLESSINGS

Many people move house in the spring, and some like to have a blessing for their new home. An old one I have often used is:

> *Who comes to me, I keep*
> *Who goes from me, I free*
> *Yet against all I stand*
> *Who do not carry my key.*

As an inscription over a doorway, with three pine cones hanging loose to blow in the wind, this is hard to beat. If you feel in need of more, here is another old threshold blessing.

> *Hang an ash bough over the door*
> *Fill your pockets with iron nails*
> *Carry always a leaf of mullein.*

But say these words against the worst:
'I stand . . . In Circles of Light . . . That Nothing . . . May Cross.'

CANDLE LORE

If sparks come from the wick, strangers will come to your door.
If you light a candle from the fire, you may expect to die in poverty.
A candle left to burn out brings bad luck. This last is a pity, because we always leave our special candles to burn out after a rite. Perhaps it is different if they are left on purpose.

An Imbolc Spell

Cold Winter is gone, the snow will thaw,
The badger stirs within the Earth.
We sing the Goddess back once more
To give the land its own re-birth.
The snowdrop comes, the robin sings,
Come now the Maiden.
And with one voice
In spring and love and Goddess we rejoice.

An Imbolc Carol

We dance the Ring of Imbolc
We dance the round of spring
We dance tonight to invoke
The hope that it will bring.

Casting A Circle

This can be used when casting a circle. It was written by a friend.

Hearken to the Words of Power, Used at the appointed hour
Time and space apart shall be, Things of wonder shall we see.
Circle pure, most clear and bright Conjured here by all our might.

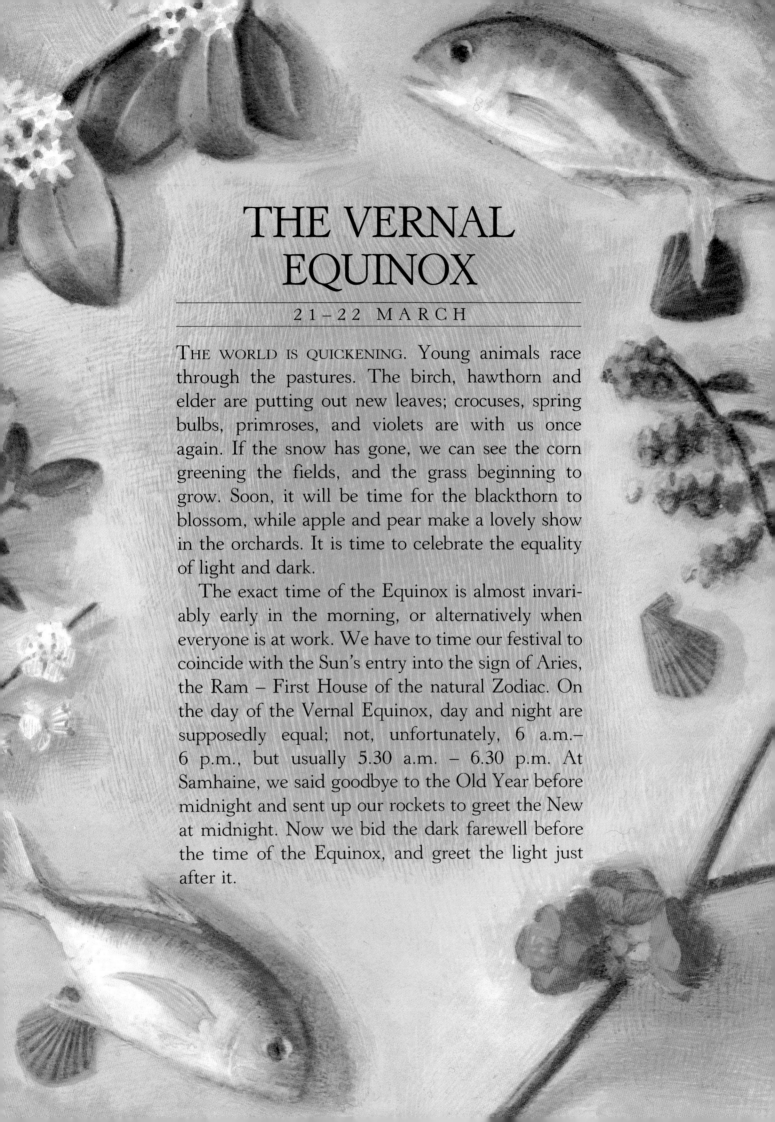

THE VERNAL EQUINOX

21–22 MARCH

THE WORLD IS QUICKENING. Young animals race through the pastures. The birch, hawthorn and elder are putting out new leaves; crocuses, spring bulbs, primroses, and violets are with us once again. If the snow has gone, we can see the corn greening the fields, and the grass beginning to grow. Soon, it will be time for the blackthorn to blossom, while apple and pear make a lovely show in the orchards. It is time to celebrate the equality of light and dark.

The exact time of the Equinox is almost invariably early in the morning, or alternatively when everyone is at work. We have to time our festival to coincide with the Sun's entry into the sign of Aries, the Ram – First House of the natural Zodiac. On the day of the Vernal Equinox, day and night are supposedly equal; not, unfortunately, 6 a.m.– 6 p.m., but usually 5.30 a.m. – 6.30 p.m. At Samhaine, we said goodbye to the Old Year before midnight and sent up our rockets to greet the New at midnight. Now we bid the dark farewell before the time of the Equinox, and greet the light just after it.

WORKING WITH THE TIDES

All magic is a question of working with the tides – not only of the sea, but of nature. Think of it this way: at the precise moment of high tide the sea is neither coming nor going. You can do things up to high tide, and you can do things immediately afterwards, but both high and low tides are slack water. It is rather the same with the Moon. There is very little point in trying to work witchcraft at full Moon. She is lovely, and it is worth going out to say how much you appreciate Her light (if you can see it for clouds). But to do work which requires power is a waste of time. Work for growth should be done when the moon is waxing, including the few days before the full Moon. This way you benefit from all the power of the tide, before the slack time.

Banishing
Banishing work should be done after the full, as the Moon wanes. Banishing is always given a rather negative meaning in books on the craft, but that is silly. If I am asked to do a working to make someone better after an illness, for instance, I always begin at the beginning. Banish the ill, the problem, or the bad luck – whatever it may be – for it is a waste of time working for recovery and well-being when the person is still full of bugs.

When the Moon returns you can begin to work for growth, good health, good luck, better conditions or a better love-life. After all, no gardener would plant new bulbs or seeds in a garden choked with weeds and rubble. Clear the ground first, dig it over, let it lie a day or so, and then plant. Why try to get someone a new love, when the old one is still hanging on? Send away the old and then work for your client's happiness.

Banishing spells do not contain phrases like 'May he get lost'. We prefer to say 'May he be happy with someone else, at some other place'. And so it is with the Equinox. Work with the tide, see what you have learned through the Winter, say goodbye, and then begin the next phase.

THE VERNAL EQUINOX RITE

In some schools of witchcraft the fight between dark and light is combined with the annual fight between the oak and the holly. We don't do this, mainly because the Equinoxes were not especially important to the Old Ones. Besides, you cannot really enact the annual battle between the oak and holly when the oak has not yet put in an appearance. The Vernal Equinox rite is for the turning of the year and the *middle* of spring. It has nothing to do with winning the hand, and everything else, of the Maiden. This happens at Beltaine in our calendar, and not before.

This rite should always be done outside, preferably in a meadow. Once again, we must contact our friend the farmer and ask if we may use his land. He has been known to join us in our blessings of the fields and the new crops.

As the early morning Sun rises we stand within the circle, thinking of the season which is just passing away. We remember how the cold of winter and early spring gripped the land, and the time when night was longer than day. We think of all we learned in theory during that winter, and how we may use our new knowledge. We must put it into practice, for this is the beginning of the magical working year when we can once again work outside. It is time to take our magical feet off the mantelpiece, roll up our magical sleeves, get out into the woods and fields, and do some real work.

Just as the Sun comes up we say goodbye to the dark time. At this point two men, representing the Sun and the Dark, fight each other. It is not a long fight, but seems like an eternal struggle between two opposites. The Sun must win, if the Earth is to continue. Once the Dark has been defeated, he leaves the circle to the victorious Sun. We all raise a cry of 'Hail, God of Light. Welcome the Lord of the Sun.' We dance a merry carol, singing the song of summer to come. There is wine and honey cake, and we close our circle with a blessing on our work and a hope for the strength to do it.

THE VERNAL EQUINOX TREE

This is the season of the alder, a tree which was sacred to the ancient British God, Bran, whose head was buried beneath the White Tower and who, even now, is supposed to protect the British Isles. The famous black ravens at the Tower of London are his birds. It is said that if they ever fly away, Britain would collapse. These days, nothing is left to chance and their wings are clipped.

The alder grows near water and remains green for longer than most trees because its leaves are thick and coated with resin. Since alder wood resists water it was often used to make the piles of bridges. The Rialto Bridge in Venice is built upon such piles, as is Winchester Cathedral which stands on very marshy ground. An ancient riddle attributed to Bran is: 'What can no house ever contain?' The answer is, 'The piles on which it is built'.

Three dyes come from the alder: red from the bark, green from the flowers, and brown from the twigs. According to Robert Graves this tree was considered particularly sacred because when its wood is cut, it is white, turning scarlet as though it is bleeding. It is a fire tree, embodying the power of fire over water – just as the Sun warms the Earth after the wet, early days of spring.

THE FLOWERS OF THE SPRING

As Imbolc was a white festival, so this one is green and yellow. Everyone should bring a bunch of yellow flowers, tied tastefully with yellow ribbons to leave at the site. We use green and yellow candles and all yellow flowers: primroses, cowslips, daffodils and jonquils.

I grow primroses and cowslips specially in my garden because I do not like to pick the few still growing wild on old pastureland (it is also illegal). Remember not to put any other flowers in a vase of daffodils as they are quite poisonous to other plants.

In the language of flowers, cowslips speak of sweetness while primroses mean new love and are supposed to say, 'I may learn to love you, it is too soon to tell'. Daffodils are not so encouraging, but jonquils hope for an affirmative answer.

HERBS

Ruled by Venus, Goddess of love, heartsease is one of the first herbs to show in the spring, for it is a very hardy little plant. It is sometimes called love-in-idleness, and is used in love spells and charms. An old fable says that it was turned purple by Cupid's dart. It may be used to strengthen the heart, and was a favourite of herbalists in time gone by.

Sweet violets
The chief herb connected with this time must be the violet. It, too, is associated with Venus, and also with the element of water. According to herbal lore it provided protection against 'wykked spectyres'. Picking the first violet you see in spring will bring you good luck.

The ancient Greeks wore violets to bring them peace and sound sleep. Another old remedy speaks of weaving a chaplet of flowers and leaves; this was a cure for headaches and dizzy spells. The scent was said to soothe the temples.

VERNAL EQUINOX SYMBOLS

The month before the Equinox, from around 19 February to 20 March, falls in Pisces, the Two Fishes, whose co-rulers are Neptune and Jupiter. Because of leap years and other complicated reasons, the exact time the Sun enters each sign of the Zodiac varies slightly from year to year. Only an ephemeris can give you the correct dates.

Pisces rules the Twelfth House of the Zodiac, which governs both the subconscious and unconscious mind. It is also the house of mystical inspiration, memory, and karma or destiny. This is a good time to try past life recall, but only if you have two other people with you. Never try astral travel or any work connected to past lives by yourself. It can be frightening, and this makes for an unhappy experience. Remember that the possibility that we died peacefully in our beds in other lives is remote. It is probably much better to leave this aspect of the craft strictly alone until you are very experienced.

The Tarot card here is number 18, the Moon. This is a card symbolizing hidden knowledge, sensitivity, intuition and karma. This conjunction of the Moon and Neptune causes the very high spring tides.

MARCH HARES

All things that love the sun are out of doors,
The sky rejoices at the morning's birth,
The grass is bright and raindrops, on the moors
The hare is running races in her mirth.

WORDSWORTH

The animal most associated with March, and with witches, is the hare. A lovely creature; gentle, loving to its children, and playful. It used to be thought that male hares boxed each other to win a female, but this is a false assumption. Female hares do the boxing, fending off importunate males until they are ready to mate. Hares used to be nicknamed 'puss' because of their habit of washing like a cat.

A witch and a hare
It was always though that witches turned themselves into hares to escape their pursuers or to travel secretly to their coven meetings. This was, presumably, when it was too dangerous to fly on their broomsticks or upon ragwort stalks. When witches were about their shapechanging they were said to chant the following old rhyme:

Hare, hare, God send thee care,
I am in hare's likeness now;
But I shall be a woman even now
Hare, hare, God send thee care.

I used to work for an old man, who owned a shooting estate in Essex. Occasionally, he had to organize a shoot of the hares. They can cause a great deal of damage to cereal crops if their numbers get out of hand. He was always very reluctant to do this because he said that when shot they cried like babies. He had been a sailor for many years and was not a sentimental man, but there were tears in his eyes when he told me this.

A couple of years ago I was on my way home from work, and had decided to visit Avebury in Wiltshire. As I drove along the narrow, winding lanes I was thinking about my life, and wondering if I was doing the right thing in working to the Earth. It was a lovely evening and the corn had been harvested. I slowed down near a gate, and looked through

into the fields beyond. As I watched, a sizeable hare came through the gate, looked at the car, and began to trot up the road in front of me. About thirty yards further on a gate opened into another field to the right. She turned in here and then faced me. I stopped and said, 'Oh wise one, am I doing the right thing?'. She looked at me for some time. Her eyes were a calm amber and her black-bordered ears twitched a little. Then she nodded and loped off across the fields.

I don't know whether hares can nod, but she seemed to. Afterwards I felt that, yes, I was working in the right way for me. Going to Avebury only confirmed this, for there I found a book about hares, which I treasure to this day.

Two Love Spells For The Vernal Equinox

Of Violets and Lavender, take of each a few,
Enclose them with Myrtle of dark green hue.
Make them in a posy, small and round and bright,
You may see your true love in your dreams tonight.

If your love to you you'd bring,
Hold these in your hand in Spring
Myrtle green and violets blue,
Then will your love come to you.

An Old Charm To Honour A Tree At Vernal Equinox

When nights and days are balanced and halved
Cut from the branches March has saved
Twelve supple wands all budded green
Twist them together to weave a crown.

Summer will come and the Winter wind
Turning and turning the leaves on their stems
Then they must fall, but now in the spring
The twig is bound and the bud remains.

Hang the leaf from a sturdy limb
Of Oak or Maple, or Ash, or Elm,
Thus will the tree live long and well.

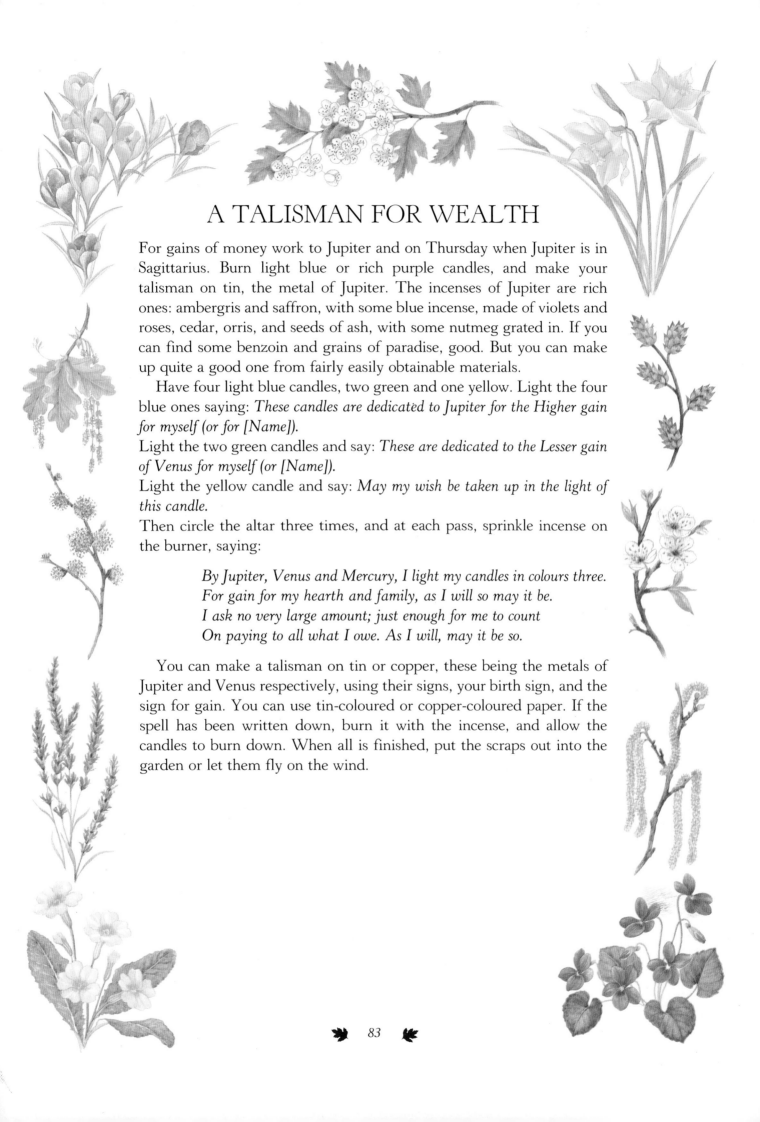

A TALISMAN FOR WEALTH

For gains of money work to Jupiter and on Thursday when Jupiter is in Sagittarius. Burn light blue or rich purple candles, and make your talisman on tin, the metal of Jupiter. The incenses of Jupiter are rich ones: ambergris and saffron, with some blue incense, made of violets and roses, cedar, orris, and seeds of ash, with some nutmeg grated in. If you can find some benzoin and grains of paradise, good. But you can make up quite a good one from fairly easily obtainable materials.

Have four light blue candles, two green and one yellow. Light the four blue ones saying: *These candles are dedicated to Jupiter for the Higher gain for myself (or for [Name]).*

Light the two green candles and say: *These are dedicated to the Lesser gain of Venus for myself (or [Name]).*

Light the yellow candle and say: *May my wish be taken up in the light of this candle.*

Then circle the altar three times, and at each pass, sprinkle incense on the burner, saying:

> *By Jupiter, Venus and Mercury, I light my candles in colours three.*
> *For gain for my hearth and family, as I will so may it be.*
> *I ask no very large amount; just enough for me to count*
> *On paying to all what I owe. As I will, may it be so.*

You can make a talisman on tin or copper, these being the metals of Jupiter and Venus respectively, using their signs, your birth sign, and the sign for gain. You can use tin-coloured or copper-coloured paper. If the spell has been written down, burn it with the incense, and allow the candles to burn down. When all is finished, put the scraps out into the garden or let them fly on the wind.

BELTAINE

MAY EVE 30 APRIL

The rising of the Sun and the running of the deer.

BELTAINE IS ONE OF the most important festivals in our calendar. By the end of April, the hawthorn is in blossom and the oak is putting out new green leaves, sometimes tipped with scarlet.

In the days when our magic was entirely seasonal, before the overlaying of the worship of the Sun, the Celebration of the Eve of the Beltaine (literally, fires of Bel, the Sky God, Welsh *tan* = Fire) happened like this. The Stag Lord, elected at birth, and now in his fourteenth year, ran with the deer. At some point, the Great Stag would scent the intruder in the herd and would turn to fight him off. The young hunter had to overcome the stag. If he were killed or wounded, there would, of course, be a substitute. When the Stag Lord returned victorious and undamaged, he mated with the Maiden, the chosen May Queen. This union between two young people trained from birth to accept their fate, or weird, was the Great Rite, in which the Goddess, represented by the Maiden, and the God, the Stag Lord, brought fertility to the land for the coming summer.

NUADA OF THE SILVER ARM

No one could lead a tribe if he had a physical disability. There is a story of the Tuatha De Danaan, the People of the goddess Dana (early matriarchal settlers in Ireland). Nuada, a young warrior, lost his right arm in battle against the monstrous Firbolg and had to stand down as leader. But over the next seven years, the Gods took pity on Nuada, for he was a great favourite, and they fashioned him a new arm made of silver and decorated with powerful runes. Thus equipped, he was allowed to take up the leadership once more, and was renamed Nuada of the Silver Arm.

A YEAR AND A DAY

It used to be said that May was an unlucky month in which to be married. This superstition dates from the time when the Church was trying to suppress the old ways, for May was a month of sexual fun and

games throughout Europe until the Reformation, after which, anyone foolish enough to deck their homes with may blossom was likely to be taken up for a witch.

In days gone by, men and women did not vow to live together until death. Ancient man was, perhaps, wise enough to know that this is not always possible. He probably did not know that after seven years, every cell in the body has been changed, so that one is not the same person at all. So at a special place, a long barrow, cromlech, or even a stone with a hole in it, a couple would hand-fast themselves on May morning. After a year and a day they might choose to continue to live together, or simply go their separate ways.

These arrangements were typical of matriarchal societies, and there were no problems about any children of such unions. Children belonged to their mothers, and everything passed through the female line. In a matriarchy there was no such concept as illegitimacy; this stigma appeared only with the advent of patriarchal societies, when power switched dramatically from the female to the male line and every man decided that he needed to know that his sons were his own.

THE RITES OF BELTAINE

We used to do this rite in a very old place, in a bend of a fast-flowing river. There were rings of trees there, firstly of birch, then holly and oak, and an ancient apple orchard. Willow and alder grew on the river bank, symbolizing respectively the Goddess and the God (Bran in this case). Most magical of all was an apple tree which grew right in the middle of the orchard. Half dead and half alive, this tree represented the two halves of the year.

Beltaine fight

Two men, representing the Holly and Oak Lords, fight each other for the hand of the Maiden, who after her mating, became the Mother and will bring forth the following spring. After this fight, when he is beaten, the Holly Lord retires with his hounds to the Wild Wood to rest until he is recalled at Samhaine.

One year we had a particularly dramatic Herne, clad in black leather and wearing a magificent set of antlers. He stood at the entrance to the circle of logs which he had built in the orchard. He challenged our right to enter and announced his name and titles. He demanded who would fight him for the hand of the Maiden. The Oak Lord, new to the part and appalled by the sight before him, completely lost his nerve. We could do nothing to make him stand and fight, so we had to choose a new combatant. Another year, the fight became so fierce that both combatants fell into the river, which considerably cooled their ardour.

Welcoming the summer

After witnessing the fight, we go home to a bowl of steaming hot punch, and sit through the short night making chaplets and decorations for the tree. On one occasion, as we returned for the morning rite, I was talking to someone just behind me. Hearing stifled giggles from further back, I turned, only to find that I was being escorted by a pair of old cart horses. The field was part of a retirement home for them. They seemed to know what was going on, for they, and several others, came all the way to the orchard and stood outside the circle. At the end of the rite they accompained us back to the gate; they too, had welcomed in the summer.

May Day, first day of summer
We've been out in the woods all night, gathering in the May.

KIPLING

At one time, May morning was greeted all over Europe with a foot stamping dance. The ONE-two-three rhythm woke up the Earth, ready for summer. In Cornwall they still do this; perhaps this is why they have better summers in this south-western county than the rest of Britain.

Following the old ways, we go out early and find our specially chosen hawthorn, the one which has most blossom. Wearing our chaplets of flowers, we dance round it and sing the summer in. We have a piper and drummer, and sing all the way there and back.

The midday rite
The midday rite looks like a series of games, but has a very serious underlying meaning. Each person taking part must bring along something he no longer uses to represent a part of himself that he wishes to be rid of. We always advise anyone taking part to make comprehensive notes afterwards about how he felt before, during, and after. This should include any dreams that might provide added illumination or inspiration.

Down by the great oak tree the Bel fires have already been prepared. Singing we begin the rite by running between the two fires, casting away everything we no longer need. We ask for a blessing upon all we will do throughout the summer months. Everyone is blessed with dew.

Welcoming the elements
We welcome the four elements, picturing them as the gentle things of Earth. Wind in the trees, the sweet scent of hawthorn and elder drifting on the air, and the sight of birds drifting upon currents of air conjure up the element of the east, air.

In the south, the place of fire, we give thanks for the fires which warm us in the cold months, the Sun which makes things grow, and the cleansing fires which destroy unwanted influences or belongings.

Water, in the western quarter of the circle, is found in the gentle spring rains, natural springs and wells, and dewdrops.

Finally, for the element of earth in the north we give thanks for everything that is beginning to grow, the scent of flowers, and all the animals now bringing forth young.

BELTAINE GAMES

This Beltaine game was devised by Steve Harrill-Morris. Centuries ago, men hunted dangerous wild boars to prove their manhood and feed their tribes. There are no longer any wild boars in Britain: besides, sausages are not nearly so wild and they haven't got tusks. You can obtain a wild boar variety.

To play Hunt the Sausage, several sausages must be hidden in the long grass. The men of the group must seek them out, greeting each discovery with glad cries and returning in triumph to the Beltaine fires.

Meanwhile, the women arrange cakes and wine in the space between the fires. Each women circles the fire, and as she completes the round she steps over the cakes and wine saying, 'I am formed in beauty, in power, and in love'. Once each has said this, she can continue circling the fires but this time she may say anything that comes into her head: for example, 'Water is wet'; 'The Sun is hot'; 'Fire burns'.

By this time the men should have returned; they are greeted, and join the circle. Each man is led through the fires and must jump over the cakes and wine making a declaration of some sort just like the women.

The women take the cakes and wine over to one fire, while the men take the sausages to the other. Each group says something significant about the God and Goddess, and then everyone passes once more between the fires.

Hoop and ball
The meaning of this game is lost in antiquity. The golden ball seems to be a straightforward fertility symbol; other sources say that it represents the Sun passing through the heavens.

Two people pick up a large, decorated hoop and throw a golden ball to one of the others. The ball is then thrown through the hoop to someone on the other side. It is very unlucky to drop the ball, or fail to get it through the hoop.

Once everyone has succeeded in making a clean throw, the ball is thrown into the fire by the last man. The last woman takes the hoop over to the great oak. We end this game by playing the even older game of Passing the Jug and eating the cake and sausage – which should be cooked by now. There is also a song, for this religious part of the rite cannot be done in silence.

Jumping over the stream
Luckily, the stream at the place where we do the rite is very narrow. We jump over it to give thanks for water, and make sure that there is enough to feed the land and crops during the growing months. Perhaps we sometimes do this a little too effectively, given the nature of English summer weather.

Weaving the summer

Everyone brings about twenty yards of coloured ribbon, which we attach to a hawthorn garland. This in turn is attached to the oak, as high as we can manage. Then we do the weaving dance, plaiting the ribbons together as we weave summer, warmth, and good growth into the tree.

There is music and singing, and once all the coloured ribbons have been woven together we tie them at the bottom with another, red, ribbon. Finally, we all join hands and dance – for as long as we have breath – sunwise round the tree to the familiar rhythm of ONE-two-three, and to the music of pipe and drum.

BELTAINE TREES

Naturally, the oak is all-important at Beltaine. It has long been associated with the thunder god; in the days when people had sun blinds at their windows the pulls were always carved in the shape of an acorn, to protect the house from lightning.

However, any oak that was struck by lightning was thought to be particularly blessed. People would travel for miles to take a small piece of such a tree as a powerful protective talisman.

The Druids are said to have taken their name from this tree. Certainly, they worshipped in oak groves, which the invading Romans deliberately cut down in an attempt to undermine the priests' power. The old cheer, Hip, Hip Hooray was originally part of a Druid chant to the Oak; so, too, was Hey Nonny, Nonny.

An ancient legend tells of the Battle of the Trees, when they fought mankind. The oak's name in this legend is Guardian of the Door, and it is unlikely to be a coincidence that the doors of many old castles and churches were made of its wood.

Dreaming of a great, healthy oak tree was considered to be very lucky. If there were acorns growing on it, these foretold children who would cause their parents to be very proud of then.

Trees of the Goddess

There is a choice here between the willow and the may tree, or hawthorn. The graceful willow is thought to bring luck in love, while the may tree has ancient links with fertility. It was associated with the Roman cult of Flora, Goddess of spring, whose rather wild May Day festival was called the Floralia. The ancient Greeks propitiated the White Goddess dwelling within the tree with five torches, made from hawthorn wood, before settling down to feasting and general merrymaking.

BELTAINE ANIMAL

Pigs used to be fed on acorns and beech mast, and so belong to the oak tree by association. They are, however, a powerful Goddess totem and were often used as such; there are many depictions of them on Pictish carved stones.

Apart from being the most intelligent domesticated animal, they have the great distinction of never fouling their sleeping quarters; anyone saying 'Dirty pig' is quite wrong. Pigs are supposed to smell the wind, and if they run about with straw in their mouths, there will soon be windy weather.

Old country lore says that they should be killed only when the Moon is waxing, or the meat will shrink when it is cooked. My grandfather said that they should never be slaughtered on a Monday, which is sacred to the Moon. Pigs used to be protected from witches on May morning; little crosses of birch and rowan were put over their sties to keep them safe.

BELTAINE SYMBOLS

Beltaine falls in Taurus, which is a fixed Earth sign, ruled by Venus and the Moon. With these two signs and the Bull, it shows fertility indeed. Taurus is the Second House of the Natural Zodiac, a house of material wealth. The Moon is in exaltation, which means its influence is strong and most positive, as it passes through this sign.

The Egyptian Gods associated with this time are Osiris the King, and Hathor often represented as a cow, echoing Taurus.

Its Tarot card is number 5, the Hierophant or High Priest. Vav is the Hebrew equivalent of the English 'and' so is a link between two things. He joins things together – man and woman, day and night, war and peace. Triumphant and eternal intelligence is the meaning of this card. It also means intuition (literally inner tuition), so a mental expansion would be looked for.

MAY DAY CHANTS

This should be chanted on the way to the early morning rite:
Holly, Oak and Hawthorn, Hip, Hip Hooray,
Round we go to greet our Maiden on this May Day.

A general May Day blessing:
Oak and May
Upon this day
Will both heed
Those in need

AN ESBAT CHANT

On the night when the Moon is full
To the Esbat we hear the call;
To come, to dance, to sing that all
May be free and strong and tall.

Round the circle we dance by three
So our Goddess we may see;
In her light our rite we do
To dedicate ourselves to You.

SPELLS

TO CURE A STY

An old cure for a sty in the eye was to stroke it with the tail of a tortoisehell cat – still attached, one presumes. This was only effective in the month of May. While stroking, you should say:

I poke thee, I don't poke thee,
I poke the queff that's under thee,
O Qualyway, O Qualyway.

FOR GENERAL HEALTH AND HAPPINESS

Oak is the Sun Lord, Maiden is the May,
Take away our pains and woes on this May Day.
Oak is the Sun Lord, He will give us strength
He will take away our fears for the Summer's length.
Hawthorn is the Maiden, She will give us peace
From the woe of aching heart, she will bring release.
Oak Lord and Maiden, Hip, Hip Hooray
Round we go to greet them both, on this May Day.

FOR PERSONAL AND GENERAL HEALING

Beltaine fires we sing, we sing
With this poppet, Health I bring
To one who pines in pain and sorrow
Beltaine fires, heal her tomorrow.

Oak and May we come to greet,
Merry here again we meet.
May those who pine in pain and sorrow
By Oak and May be healed tomorrow.

Oak and May and Beltaine fire
In these we know but one desire
May all good people on the Earth
Come to Love and Health and Mirth.

SUMMER SOLSTICE
& MIDSUMMER DAY

21 JUNE & 24 JUNE

THE SUN HAS REACHED the peak of his strength, and after this day will dwindle. There is a feeling of sadness as we know the Sun will gradually lose heat and brightness as the months pass. Once again the year has turned, and the great wheel goes on.

Many people forget that there are two separate rites at this time: Summer Solstice (21 June), and Midsummer Day (24 June) – rather like the separate festivals at mid-winter. Some even remark that the Solstice is the beginning of summer. I know the English climate is a little odd, but summer lasts longer than a week, although sometimes it may not seem like it.

Perhaps the best-known Summer Solstice festival in Britain today is performed by modern Druids at Stonehenge, the famous stone circle on Salisbury Plain. In Ancient Britain the Druids worshipped in oak groves, not stone circles. Stonehenge was, in all probability, a star temple where initiates went to study the movement of the stars. The impressive ancient monument at Avebury, in Wiltshire, was the great Sun temple of the Old Ones, and is a far more important site for this reason.

Modern Druids wait at Stonehenge for the Sun to rise over the Hele stone on Midsummer morning, but it never has; not once in five thousand years. What it actually does do is set between the opposite trilithon at mid-winter (below). Every time I have been to Stonehenge, a thick ridge of cloud has obscured the eastern horizon. By the time the Sun is visible, it is well up in the sky, and nowhere near the Hele stone.

THE SOLSTICE RITES

We celebrate the Solstice with three rites: a dawn rite for a very few, a midday rite; and a much larger, open rite in the evening. This last is attended by anyone who wishes to come and join us – pagans, witches, magicians or what you will. Afterwards there is a party and a barbecue.

The rites of dawn and midday

The dawn rite is always a short rite, and takes place on a hill from which we can see the Sun rising in the east (actually north-east). We make our circle, and after setting the quarters stand facing the east. We greet the Sun as He comes up, and dance sunwise round the circle.

We ask Bel, the Sun, to bless the earth with warmth and light so that the crops may make a good harvest. We thank Him for shining on us, and are sad that His strength will now begin to wane. Yet we know that the best of the summer follows the Solstice, just as the worst winter weather follows the Winter Solstice. Half the Summer has already gone, but we ask that the time between now and Lughnasad (2 August) will be hot and sunny. I ask a little private blessing on the cricket to be played.

At midday we return, and bless the Sun in His height, returning home to prepare for the rite at sunset.

The sunset rite

Everyone is asked to bring flowers and a piece of fruit. The fruit should be a native variety and preferably red, such as cherries or strawberries. Oranges and pineapples are not suitable, unless you are celebrating in California or Africa.

Fires and outdoor flares have been lit, and the cauldron has been set in the middle of the circle, along with some honey cake, and golden wine. At the centre of the circle a priest and priestess kneel, touching fingertips over the cauldron. They are preparing the place, and concentrating their energies on the rite to come.

Another couple are the Guardians at the gate, greeting each participant as he or she enters the circle. Each person is presented with a ribbon by the Guardian of the opposite sex, and places his or her offering of fruit in a large wooden bowl held by the female Guardian. Everyone walks sunwise, or deosil, round the circle and the Quarter Officers take their places. Now the priestess goes round the circle collecting the flowers in the cauldron, and thanking each person for their contributions. She places this, and the full fruit bowl in the circle's centre and we are ready to begin.

The priest, or Officer of the Sun, states the purpose of our gathering:

> *Good people, this is the Summer Solstice, the Longest Day, when our Lord the Sun has reached His full strength . . .*

When his speech is ended, he introduces the dance. This is our old friend, the weaving dance.

Meanwhile, the priestess greets the Earth Mother. She praises Her crops and flowers, and describes the many shades of green which are seen in Her gown at this time of year. She talks about where we may look for Her: in the raindrops, the rivers, the rainbow and the honeysuckle. Our dance and her speech come to an end and we ask that life may always be renewed.

The bowl of fruit is passed around; each person takes two pieces, one for themselves and one to return to the Earth as an offering. We hand round the cup of golden wine, and the plate of honey cakes.

The rite is ended; it is time for feasting. We usually go back to my home and have a party in the garden lit by flares. There is a barbecue, lots of salad and plenty of fruit.

THE MIDSUMMER RITE

This is always a very private affair which takes place at midday. It is an effective and special rite for the land, and those who serve and protect it.

Several years ago I found a particularly suitable place to hold this rite. It was surrounded by oak, ash, and thorn, and sometimes contains a 'fairy ring'. An old belief says that, if you're lucky, you may see fairies wherever you find an oak, ash, and thorn growing together. A 'fairy ring' is a ridge of darker, richer grass formed by toadstools or mushrooms, which sometimes grow in a circle, and has long been linked with magic and the little people.

We stand in the form of a pentacle, the five-pointed star. Each point represents one of the four elements, while the fifth symbolizes spirit. Everyone holds sprigs of oak, ash and thorn, while reciting Shakespeare's speech about the fairies from *A Midsummer Night's Dream.* Many of Shakespeare's plays contain magical references; he clearly knew a good deal about magic.

We always dedicate this rite to Puck, the Old One, as Rudyard Kipling called him. In England you should always concentrate on this being when working for the good of the land. Finally, we lie down in the meadow grass to meditate on whatever it is we particularly want to put right.

A SHAKESPEAREAN SPELL

One of the most famous spells in literature was cast by the Three Witches in *Macbeth,* (Act IV, scene I). But few people realize that the gruesome ingredients were mainly old country names for herbs. Both hairy mullein and woolly faverel were known as wool of bat; the grease from the murderer's gibbet is felonwort or bittersweet; Jew's liver is Jew's ear or cuckoo-pint; gall of goat is goat's rue; eye of newt is rocket; while tongue of dog is obviously hound's tongue. The passage also mentions hemlock and yew.

But even when the ingredients are translated, they would still make you pretty sick – even though they are not as horrific as they first seem.

SUMMER SYMBOLS

Summer Solstice usually falls on the cusp between Gemini, The Twins, and Cancer, the Crab. Gemini, ruled by Mercury, governs the Third House of communication. This house is also concerned with brothers and sisters, and short journeys. Mercury or Hermes was the messenger of the Gods and is usually depicted with winged sandals on his feet. So this is a good time to be sociable, or contact people you haven't seen for a while.

By Midsummer Day, the Sun has entered Cancer, ruled by the Moon. This sign governs the Fourth House, which has to do with the home, family, and stability. The Moon represents our emotional responses to these things, which we carry with us wherever we go – just like the crab. Traditionally, and most appropriately, the Fourth House also rules the land itself.

The Tarot card here is number 7, The Chariot. This card suggests movement, both physical and mental. It is connected with communication (Gemini), and a need to use intuition to look beyond immediate circumstances (Cancer).

SOLSTICE SUPERSTITIONS

On Midsummer Day, decorate the house with birch twigs and roses.

It is very unlucky to hear a cuckoo calling on Midsummer Day; she is not supposed to sing on this day.

When gnats dance up and down good weather is on the way. But if they rush about and sting, a prolonged period of rain is coming.

If the first butterfly you see on Midsummer Day is white, you will eat white bread for the rest of the year. If brown, you will have to survive on inferior brown bread. Of course, this was written when white bread was a luxury few could afford – and no-one realized the healthy qualities of the brown variety.

ST JOHN AND THE SOLSTICE

In the Christian calendar, St John the Baptist was born at Midsummer. All the old incantations to Bel, the Sun, were re-dedicated to St John by the early Church fathers.

St John's wort is, according to the herbalist Culpeper, a universal cure-all. But it has one serious drawback; too much can make you allergic to sunshine – a quality it shares with bergamot.

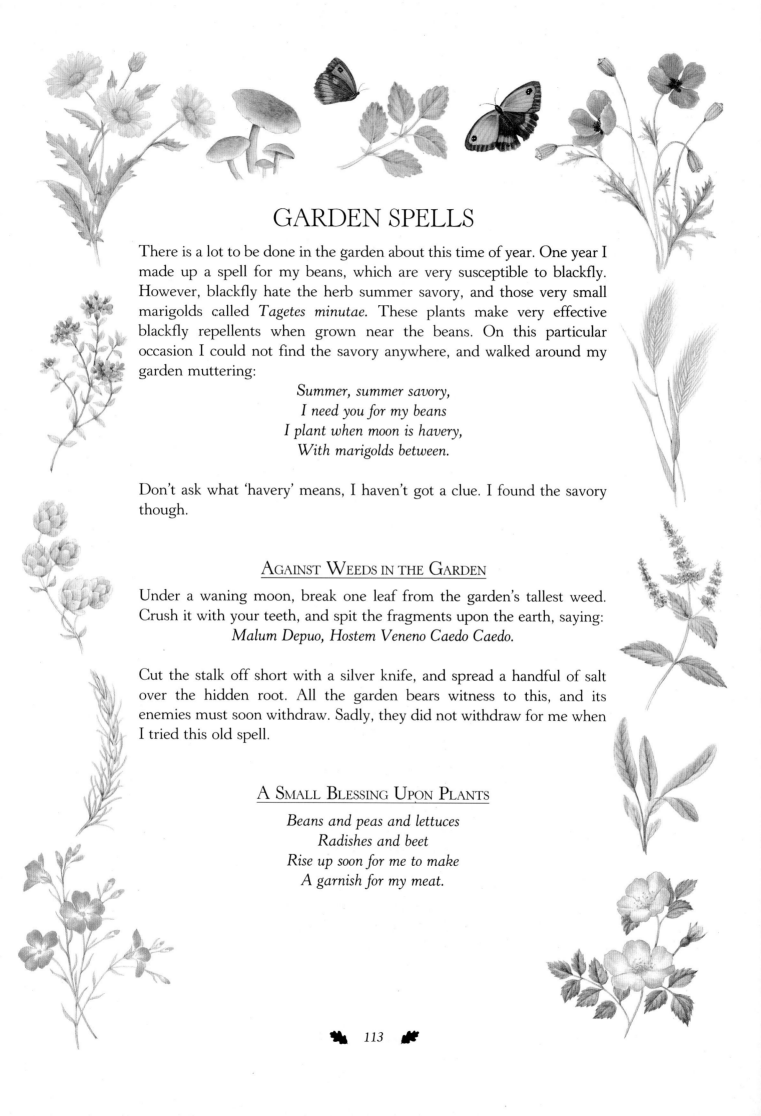

GARDEN SPELLS

There is a lot to be done in the garden about this time of year. One year I made up a spell for my beans, which are very susceptible to blackfly. However, blackfly hate the herb summer savory, and those very small marigolds called *Tagetes minutae*. These plants make very effective blackfly repellents when grown near the beans. On this particular occasion I could not find the savory anywhere, and walked around my garden muttering:

> *Summer, summer savory,*
> *I need you for my beans*
> *I plant when moon is havery,*
> *With marigolds between.*

Don't ask what 'havery' means, I haven't got a clue. I found the savory though.

AGAINST WEEDS IN THE GARDEN

Under a waning moon, break one leaf from the garden's tallest weed. Crush it with your teeth, and spit the fragments upon the earth, saying:
> *Malum Depuo, Hostem Veneno Caedo Caedo.*

Cut the stalk off short with a silver knife, and spread a handful of salt over the hidden root. All the garden bears witness to this, and its enemies must soon withdraw. Sadly, they did not withdraw for me when I tried this old spell.

A SMALL BLESSING UPON PLANTS

> *Beans and peas and lettuces*
> *Radishes and beet*
> *Rise up soon for me to make*
> *A garnish for my meat.*

A Solstice Herbal Chant

Thyme and sage for sore throats,
Rosemary to darken hair,
Bergamot to make a tea,
Flax for me to wear.

Cecily for sour fruit,
Lemon balm a cake,
Chive to mix with salad and egg,
Mint a thirst to slake.

The monks of old with loving care
Grew herbs and gave poor folk a share,
And cottage gardens still are found
Where Nature's medicines abound.

A Spell For Sunrise On Summer Solstice

When June is ripe and days are full
And Sun comes early to claim His throne
Walk before dawn to a silent height
And set three stones in an Eastern line.

Stand behind them while His light
Is rising over the distant land,
When he is in the Eastern sky,
Offer these words and understand.

Sun of the Year, I move the Earth
To greet Thy Sign, and set myself
To honour Thee in Earth's design.

Perfect the stones to mark His Face,
Follow their shadow twelve short paces,
Pluck some leaf for an amulet,
And wear on your coat, lest you forget.

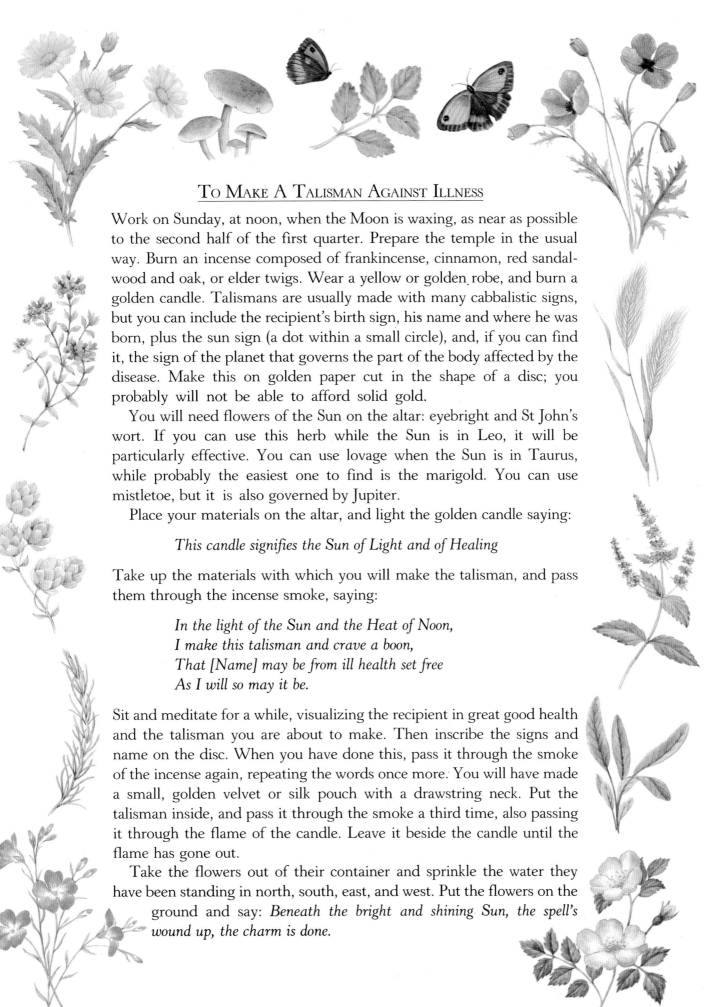

To Make A Talisman Against Illness

Work on Sunday, at noon, when the Moon is waxing, as near as possible to the second half of the first quarter. Prepare the temple in the usual way. Burn an incense composed of frankincense, cinnamon, red sandalwood and oak, or elder twigs. Wear a yellow or golden robe, and burn a golden candle. Talismans are usually made with many cabbalistic signs, but you can include the recipient's birth sign, his name and where he was born, plus the sun sign (a dot within a small circle), and, if you can find it, the sign of the planet that governs the part of the body affected by the disease. Make this on golden paper cut in the shape of a disc; you probably will not be able to afford solid gold.

You will need flowers of the Sun on the altar: eyebright and St John's wort. If you can use this herb while the Sun is in Leo, it will be particularly effective. You can use lovage when the Sun is in Taurus, while probably the easiest one to find is the marigold. You can use mistletoe, but it is also governed by Jupiter.

Place your materials on the altar, and light the golden candle saying:

This candle signifies the Sun of Light and of Healing

Take up the materials with which you will make the talisman, and pass them through the incense smoke, saying:

In the light of the Sun and the Heat of Noon,
I make this talisman and crave a boon,
That [Name] may be from ill health set free
As I will so may it be.

Sit and meditate for a while, visualizing the recipient in great good health and the talisman you are about to make. Then inscribe the signs and name on the disc. When you have done this, pass it through the smoke of the incense again, repeating the words once more. You will have made a small, golden velvet or silk pouch with a drawstring neck. Put the talisman inside, and pass it through the smoke a third time, also passing it through the flame of the candle. Leave it beside the candle until the flame has gone out.

Take the flowers out of their container and sprinkle the water they have been standing in north, south, east, and west. Put the flowers on the ground and say: *Beneath the bright and shining Sun, the spell's wound up, the charm is done.*

LAMMAS – LUGHNASAD

1–2 AUGUST

THIS IS A TIME OF thanksgiving, for we are celebrating the beginning of the harvest. We mourn the soul of John Barleycorn, who dies for our good.

Lammas comes from the Saxon word for the Feast of Bread, *Hlaf-mass*. It was a major harvest festival all over Europe; Ceres, Demeter and Juno Augusta were all names of the Goddess who presided over the ripening harvest. To us, Lammas is still the Lady's rite when the first loaf of bread is made from the first sheaf of the year's harvest.

Lammas Eve, 1 August, is the festival of the God Lugh, the Celtic God who gave his name to London – originally Lugdunum. This festival celebrated the death and resurrection of Lugh as grain God. Similarly, we commemorate John Barleycorn's death and the sacrifice of the harvest for the good of his children.

Our first rite, on Lammas Eve, is usually done by the men. They tell of the growth and decay of the Lord of the Sun who, having given us His strength, is now cut down.

This is a solemn ritual, for everyone thinks of the sadness which comes with ultimate growth. We know that now harvest is inevitable.

A Lughnasad Chant

John Barleycorn is cut down dead, it is His time to die
The Sun that warmed our summer days no longer is so high.
We praise Him and our Goddess fair, we thank Him for the corn,
We gather in the harvest now, and leave the fields forlorn.

THE RITE OF LAMMAS

Lammas is the Lady's rite. We perform it in the circle as a thanksgiving for the harvest, and a blessing upon the Earth Mother for Her bounty. We have made a loaf from the first gleanings in the fields, and brewed beer – not from this season's hops, I'm afraid, but from a kit. There is still a great deal for us to harvest. For the next two months there will be apples, elderberries, crab apples, blackberries, hops, and sloes to pick and gather.

At this time of year we also try to consolidate our practical work. During the cold, winter months we shall reflect upon everything we have done during the warm weather; there is always more to learn. We also need to prepare ourselves with plenty to keep us busy so that we don't waste that precious commodity, time.

The Lady's rite

The circle is formed, and the quarters have been raised. The priestess speaks:

> 'This is the beginning of harvest. At this time long ago,
> our ancestors went out into the fields to collect the first
> ripened ears of corn.
> These were brought back to the tribe with great rejoicing,
> and the women of the tribe ground the seeds to make the
> first bread of the season.
> This loaf was held to be particularly sacred, and a festival
> of the first loaf was consecretated. The whole tribe was
> given of this, the first fruits of the gathering.
> Today we celebrate also, and we acknowledge the part
> played by the Lord in His three aspects.
> We remember also our younger brothers in life. They,
> too, are beginning to collect their stores for the coming
> winter, as the migrant birds leave us.
> The summer has been cool and wet (or hot and sunny),
> yet Our Lady Mother, the Earth, has given us abundance.
> The days are getting shorter, and we know that after the
> harvest is completed autumn will be well advanced, and
> with it the last of the fruit and berries.'

The priest says:
> 'The corn is ripe and the grass is lush and green. We, the
> Children of the Goddess, look forward to the harvest. The
> great wheel is turning towards the mists of autumn, and
> we gather in the bountiful fruit of the Earth as we begin to
> gather in ourselves.
> We pray for good weather now to gather in the harvest
> standing in the fields, for soft winds to dry the grains.
> Let us give love and praise to the Lord and the Lady who
> have shown their love for us.'

The priest then invokes the Goddess into the priestess, saying
'Hear the words of the Lady.'

The Goddess speaks through the priestess, saying:
> 'My beloved children, listen to the words I whisper in the corn. Watch for my cloak of green moving in the long grass of the meadow like the waves of the sea.
>
> My Earth teems with life; food grows in abundance, birds have left their nests, young animals born in spring are in their strength – already learning the lessons to carry them through the winter.
>
> The rivers teem with fish in their prime. Herbs, fruits, and nuts will soon have given of their best, to die away in the long sleep of winter.
>
> As the wheel spins they blossom, seed and die – to be born again.
>
> The dying of summer may make you sad, but always remember my promise: spring follows winter as day follows night, and in order to grow you must let go, for you cannot stand still while all else moves.
>
> The greenwood is full of birdsong, and small creatures busy about their lives. And there our Lord Herne waits until his return at Samhaine. The Sun still warms our days, and gives us time to gather in.
>
> I am She who was, and will be, yet my love grows with each turn of the wheel.'

A moment of stillness . . .

The priestess invokes the Lord into the priest, who says:
> 'Hear me, good people. My forests are full of melody as the trees sway in the wind, and the birds sing. Squirrels begin their search for nuts; badgers and small creatures play beneath the harvest Moon. Owls cry in the still, warm night and we hear the first tentative calls of the vixen and the dog fox. Soon the woods will ring to the sound of the rut.
>
> Summer is nearing its end, and my days in the Greenwood are nearly done. Soon the autumn gales will bare the branches of the trees, and it will be time for me to return as Hunter and protector of my people.
>
> Store up the harvest, draw strength from the Sun, and be ready to greet me at Samhaine.'

Closing the rite

The priest leads everyone seven times round the circle. He concentrates on drawing strength into them, and into himself. We all share the wine, saying, 'We drink to the harvest, and the abundance of Earth'. Then we pass round the first loaf, and the barley cake, saying, 'We share the first fruits of the harvest, and give thanks to the Mother'.

> Let us dwell on the Bounty of the Goddess.
> Let us think on the strength of the Lord.

Finally, everyone walks widdershins three times round the circle. The rite is ended.

THE LAMMAS TREE

We are in the time of the hazel tree, ruled by Mercury, and ninth in the tree alphabet of Ancient Britain. Each tree had a special name and meaning, and the Old Ones sent messages to each other composed of the leaves arranged like letters of the alphabet. Perhaps this is the origin of the language of flowers, so popular in Victorian times.

The hazel tree was called Coll by the Celts; nine hazels grew over the legendary Connla's well, producing flowers and fruit simultaneously.

When their nuts fell into the well they were eaten by the salmon which lived there. The number of nuts the fish ate were recorded in the spots on their skin. This fish was held to be very wise by the Celts.

Hazels are still linked with water; forked twigs from this tree are used by water diviners. Magicians' wands, too, always used to be made from one-year-old hazel wood. Nowadays, people seem to have a different wand for each day of the week and for every possible occasion.

According to the old herbalists, hazel nut kernels crushed with mead or honey are soothing for an old cough. They were also considered an aphrodisiac when combined with purslane, jasmine, periwinkle, and anemone. The nuts are reputed to be good for a weak heart.

An old country saying about hazel nuts:

If the nutshells are thick, the winter will be bleak
If the nutshells are thin, the winter will be mild.

THE LUGHNASAD PLANT

Barley is the appropriate plant. It belongs to the element of Earth, and is ruled by Venus – another name for the Mother Goddess. A corn dolly, which is traditionally made from barley straw, should be hung up in the home to attract health and wealth.

The Mother Goddess, Demeter, also known as the Wise One of Earth and Sea, once· sent her lover Triptolemus down into the world of men with a bag of barley seed. The young God's name actually means 'three ploughings', and he is supposed to have taught agriculture.

Thousands of years ago there was a barley cult. The God, Cronos, had been castrated and so was no longer fertile. Therefore he was sacrificed with a sickle. His blood, symbolized by scarlet poppies, spilt upon the ground to bring fertility to the Earth. Celtic warriors always carried small sickles with them into battle. They castrated their prisoners with these symbolic weapons.

Barley cakes and the Sun

Our barley cakes and new bread are marked with an ancient Sun sign, the eight-armed cross. The Sun cults did not think of the number seven, a number sacred to the Moon, as being of much significance. Eight was their sacred number because it was arrived at by multiplying 2 by itself three times. Both Nordic runes and the Chinese book of wisdom, *The I Ching,* are based on the numbers 8 and 3.

LAMMAS SYMBOLS

Lammas and Lughnasad fall in the sign of Leo, the Lion, a fiery sign ruled by the Sun. The colour of Leo is greenish yellow, reminiscent of ripening corn. And since harvest time has just begun, this is a good time to have the Sun with us – or the crops may be ruined.

Leo governs the Fifth House of the Zodiac, the house of creativity, love affairs, pleasure, children and happy social occasions. We put our creativity into gathering in everything we need for the coming winter, including presents to be given at Winter Solstice. On a higher level, we are gathering our thoughts and generating ideas.

The Tarot card is number 8, Strength or Fortitude. This card is associated with courage, success, and faith. It also symbolizes the sacred serpent power, or cosmic electricity; this is the driving energy force behind life and the universe.

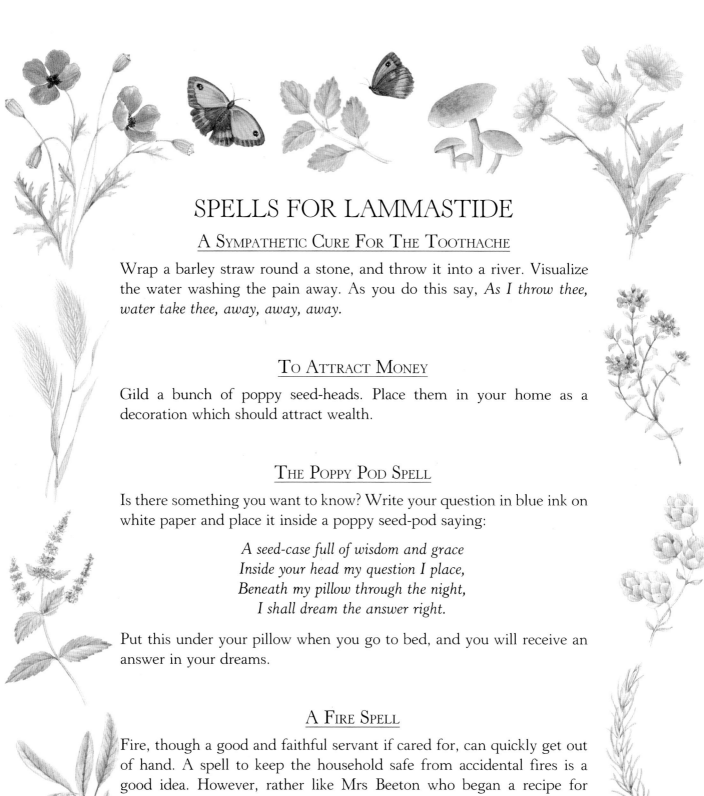

SPELLS FOR LAMMASTIDE

A Sympathetic Cure For The Toothache

Wrap a barley straw round a stone, and throw it into a river. Visualize the water washing the pain away. As you do this say, *As I throw thee, water take thee, away, away, away.*

To Attract Money

Gild a bunch of poppy seed-heads. Place them in your home as a decoration which should attract wealth.

The Poppy Pod Spell

Is there something you want to know? Write your question in blue ink on white paper and place it inside a poppy seed-pod saying:

> *A seed-case full of wisdom and grace*
> *Inside your head my question I place,*
> *Beneath my pillow through the night,*
> *I shall dream the answer right.*

Put this under your pillow when you go to bed, and you will receive an answer in your dreams.

A Fire Spell

Fire, though a good and faithful servant if cared for, can quickly get out of hand. A spell to keep the household safe from accidental fires is a good idea. However, rather like Mrs Beeton who began a recipe for jugged hare with the immortal words, 'First catch your hare', this old spell suggests that you 'First catch your salamander.'

Once you have found this elusive creature, trap him in a cave of woven willows and hurry home before he burns it. Set the salamander down near the fireplace, and cross some withies, or osier – which are like slim willow wands – in the fireplace. Set light to these twigs, then put them out quickly with freshly-drawn well water saying:

> *Salamander, Salamander, Turn Fire to Water*
> *Under this house, and over this house.*

TO PROTECT THE HOUSEHOLD

Take five hairs from a golden broom bush. Using them as tapers, carry them throughout the house asking good fortune to come as you say:

Wraiths of the House, take heart and fire.
To every chamber light I give
To every corner this breath I send
Help this house in which I live.

For added efficacy, sprinkle the floors with a mixture of orris root, tea leaves, and salt, then sweep them absolutely clean.

FOR A JOURNEY

It is sometimes quite pleasant to have a little chant or charm to mutter under your breath as you set out upon a journey. I always do so, even if I am not driving. These are addressed to the God of Going, who is Mercury: He governs travel. At one time there was a little Herm at every crossroads, and travellers would touch it for 'luck'. I will not tell you my own charm, but here are two you might find useful. Facing east say:

The journey I make is one of need,
I ask the God to pay me heed
That I may safely homeward come,
There and back when my work is done.

May the God of Going hear my call
To my going and coming no ill befall
May I drive with care and may those I meet
Be safe and careful on the street.

It might be a good idea if you did this the first time within the house, using yellow candles and Mercury incense. You could then make a talisman, rather in the same way as before. This should be done on Wednesday, and, as well as the incenses and flowers of Mercury, you should use those of Gemini. Use some lavender and rosemary; these keep you calm and give wisdom, both of which are necessary on busy roads. You can use fennel and marjoram, as well as lavender, lime, lemon and mace.

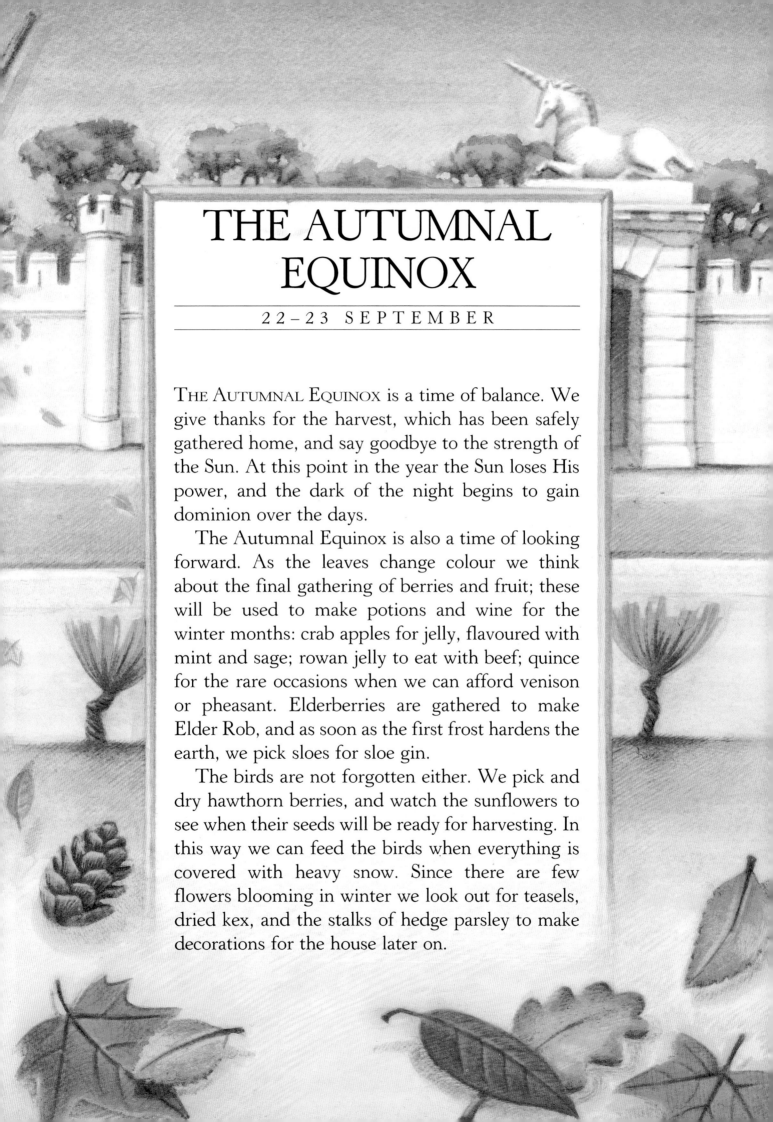

THE AUTUMNAL EQUINOX

22–23 SEPTEMBER

THE AUTUMNAL EQUINOX is a time of balance. We give thanks for the harvest, which has been safely gathered home, and say goodbye to the strength of the Sun. At this point in the year the Sun loses His power, and the dark of the night begins to gain dominion over the days.

The Autumnal Equinox is also a time of looking forward. As the leaves change colour we think about the final gathering of berries and fruit; these will be used to make potions and wine for the winter months: crab apples for jelly, flavoured with mint and sage; rowan jelly to eat with beef; quince for the rare occasions when we can afford venison or pheasant. Elderberries are gathered to make Elder Rob, and as soon as the first frost hardens the earth, we pick sloes for sloe gin.

The birds are not forgotten either. We pick and dry hawthorn berries, and watch the sunflowers to see when their seeds will be ready for harvesting. In this way we can feed the birds when everything is covered with heavy snow. Since there are few flowers blooming in winter we look out for teasels, dried kex, and the stalks of hedge parsley to make decorations for the house later on.

THE AUTUMNAL EQUINOX RITE

Everyone is asked to bring a candle, fixed securely in a jar of sand or soil. They are also requested to hunt out some sprigs from an oak, pine cones, autumn flowers, an ear of wheat, oats, or barley and a piece of fruit. This gathering should be done with care, for it represents each person's token offering to the Gods.

Altar and fire

We have an altar, where a bowl of flowers in clear spring water has been placed. This symbolizes the Mother, and is surrounded by berries and fruit. A fire is lit outside the magic circle at its southern point, representing the Sun which is leaving us.

The quarters are set as usual, and each person walks round the circle and casts his or her offering into the fire as a token of thanks for blessings received through the summer.

Circles

After this part of the rite the women form an inner circle, and progress around the circle widdershins. Meanwhile the men stand in an outer circle and move sunwise round the perimeter. We all chant:

> *The wheel turns on to autumn time,*
> *The Gods are strong, and in their prime.*
> *We give our love and thanks anew*
> *O God and Goddess, praise to you.*
> *O power bring the balance in*
> *As the wheel retains its spin.*

There is more, but since this constitutes a special spell we have cast, I shall not give it here, for that would dissipate its power.

Finally, we raise our hands to the sky, visualizing power and balance. This picture must be held firmly in everyone's mind until the priestess finally says, 'The thing is done, so will it be'. We share cakes and dark, red wine; the rite is closed.

TRADITIONAL HARVEST GAME

This game, which is actually a fertility rite, is a boisterous but authentic addition to our rite. It was prepared by Steve Harrill-Morris, who has kindly allowed me to include it.

Ideally, there should be equal numbers of men and women. Children enjoy taking part too. My grand-daughter usually has to be the token female in the male party because wherever her brother goes, she goes too. You will need to wear old clothes, and bring something to change into afterwards. Towels are also an essential part of the equipment.

Find a place to represent 'Home', where there is a low wall or perhaps a large rock which can be used as a table. It is best if this table can be approached under cover from several directions. This place is secret; the men must not be told where it is, for part of the game is trying to find it.

Killing the Bright Lord

A sheaf of corn, decorated with a red ribbon, is taken to a place some distance away from 'Home', out of sight and hearing.

The men go off to 'Kill the Bright Lord', represented by the sheaf. They carry copious amounts of ale, and an old sickle – which we found in one of my outhouses before they were demolished.

They set up the sheaf in a cleared space, and sing songs like 'John Barleycorn' in the most macho voices they can manage. Forming a ring around the sheaf, each man steps four paces from the centre; one for each winter month, and one for luck. The jug of ale is then passed round. Each man must drink before taking a throw at the sheaf. As each one throws the sickle he must say something to the God he intends to slay. This goes on until someone knocks or cuts the sheaf down.

The men then split up to attack Home, coming from as many directions as possible. This approach is silent at first, and then wild cries are heard as they reach their objective.

The cave of the Goddess

The women, meanwhile, are busy preparing the table. This represents the cave of the Goddess to which the slain hero is brought. They lay out a feast, and prepare devious deterrents for the invading men. Buckets of milk and water, and sometimes plates of crazy foam, green slime and soot are added. These delightfully messy ingredients are placed in all kinds of booby traps: buckets, paper plates and so on. You can see why a change of clothes is required.

Attacking home

Once the men have launched their attack, it is essential that they are all made as wet as possible – especially the man carrying the sheaf, for he will be the one who has cut it. This part of the game usually ends in a frontal attack, as the men pass the sheaf between themselves like a rugby ball or American football. Everyone sings:

Let us welcome home the fallen
To the Goddess all return
The seed shall fertilize the womb
So that life shall be re-born

The women defend Home with everything they can lay their hands on, until one of the men succeeds in placing the now-soaking sheaf on the table. He is designated priest for the remainder of the rite.

A harvest feast

The woman who scored the first hit becomes priestess. This couple now hang the sheaf, suitably dowsed with clean water, from a branch. They bless the food and wine (or ale), and are the first to eat and drink – uttering whatever thanks they think fit. Everyone joins in, and we get down to some serious feasting.

Balance

After the feast the sheaf is either taken down and buried, or kept until the spring – when it should form part of the Imbolc fire. Either way it must eventually return to Earth. This festival has a serious side, for it is one of balance. It points up the need for balance in the relationship between the two sexes, and their mutual dependence.

AUTUMNAL EQUINOX TREE

Some scholars, including Robert Graves, maintain that this is the time of the vine. And although it did appear regularly as a Celtic decorative motif, it is not native to the British Isles. I feel that the apple tree is more appropriate here; this tree is steeped in legend and magic.

AUTUMNAL EQUINOX HERB

The hop is a northern vine, which, like the grape, is used to make a wonderfully intoxicating brew. We use ale or beer almost as often as wine when celebrating our rites.

In spring, young hop shoots may be eaten in salad. Beer makes bread leaven quickly; I always make my fritter batter with beer because it is lighter than milk, and tastes better.

Hops, in moderation, are good for the liver. The dried flowers stuffed into a herbal pillow are a wonderful cure for insomnia. They are often put into healing sachets and powders, and do not clarify only beer. I use them to clarify many simples, potions and infusions.

THE APPLE SPELL STORY

Autumnal Equinox is always a good time to do some spells involving apples. When I took part in the television programme *Earth Magic*, I performed an apple spell, which had been specially written for me, simply as an example. I even invented an imaginary couple whom it was intended to help, although I had tried to make it clear that I don't agree with interfering in people's lives.

This spell was taken extremely seriously by the press, who wanted to learn the outcome, and I received many requests to perform it from lovelorn members of the public. I don't recommend anyone trying this spell, but here it is:

Apple, apple, Red as blood
(Here you cut the apple in half)
As two become, two hearts in one
Each one bears the sacred star
(Apples have a five-pointed star in their centres)
I call to each one from afar
A herb for her, a herb for him
(A cut is made and the herb inserted)
A touch of fire to seal it in
(Done with a taper, lit at a candle. It makes a lovely hissing sound)
Bind with the cord to make them one
(Tie round with scarlet cord)
As I will, so be it done.
(Bury the apple in the ground)

AUTUMNAL EQUINOX SYMBOLS

This rite is at the very end of Virgo, the virgin, which is ruled by Mercury, and is dominated by the self-conscious initiative, according to Case. This is one's own harvest, that which one has acquired for oneself. We are gathering in our own harvest of work and thought, as well as the harvest of the fields. Mercury rules the intellect; anything to do with learning is especially relevant with Mercury in Virgo, the Earth sign in which Mercury is exalted.

The Tarot card is The Hermit, a card of inclination and tendency rather than activity. The Hebrew word is Yod, meaning an open hand. It is the supreme will, the urge to freedom, but it could also mean a failure to face facts.

The colour for this sign is yellowish green, and its stone is the peridot.

Long ago, the apple tree was so sacred that anybody who felled one without good reason was sentenced to death. Later on, this was changed to a fine – one cow for each tree destroyed.

In Celtic mythology, the Great Tree of Munga was a combination of oak, hazel, and apple. This magic tree produced oak apples, acorns, hazel nuts and apples all at the same time. It was also a tree of sanctuary where the White Hind, a form sometimes taken by the Goddess, could shelter.

The fabled unicorn also rested beneath an apple tree, symbolizing immortality through wisdom. This beautiful mythical creature could only be tamed by a virgin. Nowadays we think of a virgin as a girl with an intact hymen. But in the old legends it meant a woman with spiritual integrity, an attribute of the Goddess – who was not a virgin in the physical sense.

The Isle of Avalon, a Celtic name for the Otherworld, also means Isle of Apples. King Arthur was taken to Avalon after his last battle. These trees bore both fruit and flower at the same time, and probably gave rise to the old saying:

A bloom on the tree when the apple is ripe
Is a sure termination of somebody's life.

Diana, Lady of Wild Creatures, was for centuries Goddess of the Sacred Grove. The two main ones were at Ephesus and Nemi; an apple tree and a deer are two symbols associated with Diana, or Artemis as she was known to the Greeks. Nemesis, called Nemhain by the Celts, also presided over holy groves, and is often portrayed with an apple branch in her hand.

AN APPLE LOVE SPELL

A genuine old charm: pick your apple when the moon has waned three days. Breathe upon its green cheek, rub it with a scarlet cloth and say:

Fire sweet and fire red
Warm the heart and turn the head.

Kiss the red half, put it in another's hand. Who holds it shall weaken; who eats it shall be yours.

To See Your Lover In A Dream

When I was a girl in Kent we used to recite this little charm whenever we found the first yarrow in flower, usually round this time of year.

Yarrow, sweet yarrow, the first I have found
In the name of the Lord I pluck thee from the ground.
As the Lord loves the Lady, so warm and so dear,
So in a dream may my lover appear.

MICHAELMAS

29 SEPTEMBER

MOST PEOPLE BELIEVE THAT George killed the dragon, but this legend has been grafted on to the much older story of Michael, Prince of Light, taming the Dragon of Knowledge.

The high, conical hills of St Michael are invariably crowned by a church, often in ruins. Such places were sacred to the Old Ones long before they were appropriated by the Church. Glastonbury Tor, Somerset, Brent Tor in Devon, and St Michael's Mount in Cornwall are some of the better-known British sites, dedicated to St Michael, and, in France, there is Mont St Michel, a twin of the Cornish hill. Most of these hills are on ley-lines, those invisible currents of Earth energy which link ancient sacred places all over the world. Any church built on a pointed hill is dedicated to St Michael.

The Bible says that Michael was given power over the heavens, and he has been equated with Primeval Eros, who created the firmament. Unlike St George, Michael does not slay the dragon but, instead, comes to terms with him. This dragon symbolizes raw energy, like the element of Fire in its unharnessed, primal form. Michael represents structure; that which brings random, chaotic energy into order.

THE MICHAELMAS RITE

At Michaelmas we see the last of the harvest. It is time to clear the ground, ready for Winter. This rite is my own. We begin by building a cairn of rocks on the site where we performed our Celtic Harvest Rite. Well to the south of the cairn we dig a fire pit, making sure that our fire will light quickly. To the west, a natural spring does very well for West, the Place of Water. A great hill rises up in the Northern Quarter of the circle, while the land is open to the east.

A seven-ringed deosil spiral is made, winding out from the centre of our cairn. Its diameter is seven times seven: forty nine feet. Finally, a sword is fixed into the cairn's centre and the preparations are complete.

The rite

As the Sun goes down we gather, in ordinary clothes, outside the spiral. Several previously selected people have gone into the trees to wait until they are called. Everyone carries an unlit candle in a glass holder.

Forming into a nine-foot circle around the cairn, we invoke the Lord and the Lady. Whoever has been chosen to be Michael leads us round the circle and into the spiral maze.

A spiral in time

As the spiral tightens, we imagine that we are travelling back into the past. By the time we have completed the maze we have arrived at the dawn of human history, when the race was without fire.

Michael's speech

Michael approaches the cairn alone. He says: *From stone comes iron. From our Stone Age we progressed to the Iron Age. The sword is in the stone.*

Here he lights a small fire at the southern base of the cairn; the larger fire is lit simultaneously outside the circle. Once it is blazing satisfactorily, he paces round to the north of the cairn, removes the sword, and brings it back to the south. Passing the blade through the flames he calls out: *Mankind has been without fire. I have purified the sword in the sacred flame. Come to the fire, each in turn, and be kindled.*

He takes a branch, or taper, and each person lights his candle from it. We take our places back in the circle, and say: *We give thanks for the gift of fire. May we always use it aright.*

The Dragon of Untamed Force

Michael leads the circle outwards without unwinding the spiral. When we are standing in the outer circle, a great roar is heard from the trees. The Dragon of Untamed Force strides forth, and engages Michael in a short, stylized physical battle. Once they realize they are evenly matched they stop. Michael says: *The Dragon of Untamed Force has been tamed.*

The Dragon says: *Long have I been ruled by chaos. Henceforward I will be the Silver Dragon of Albion. I shall give heat and light to those who ask, and I shall lend my strength to the service of the Light and of the Land, so long as this be needed.*

We return to the cairn once more, and sit in the circle while one of our number recites the story of what we have just witnessed. Then Michael leads us back widdershins, unravelling the maze, while the Dragon brings up the rear. As we go, each brings himself or herself back to the present, walking back through the maze of time until we reach the present. The wide outer circle has re-formed and we face the cairn passing round the cup of wine and a plate of oatcakes.

Closing the Rite

We give thanks to the fire, and praise to the light and the land with the power of Michael and the Silver Dragon. We say hail and farewell to the Lord and Lady. There is a short blessing, and the rite is ended.

A MICHAELMAS PATHWORKING

Close your eyes, and allow the mists to form around you. You are going back through time. Wait for the mist to change from white to orange; it will dissolve as it does so. . . .

You stand looking into a fire burning brightly in a brazier. You are in a clearing in the woods beneath a starlit sky. Behind you, a hermit's hut offers a little shelter. Before you the forest seems alive with half-heard sounds.

You are alone, save for a horse tethered off to the left. As you wait, a feeling of anticipation comes over you, and you wish that the light armour you wear was somewhat more substantial. The sword you hold trembles in your hand as the feeling grows: something is about to happen.

A light approaches from the opposite side of the clearing, as it reaches the edge you are aware only of this light. As you watch, it parts and gives the impression of a doorway into the trees beyond. This is the invitation you came for. It is your only opportunity to turn back. You hesitate. Do you really want to face what lies ahead?

An ember cracks in the brazier, and the spell cast over you loses its hold for a moment. This is what you came for. You move towards the door, and pass from the land you know into the realms that few mortals know at all, and no mortal knows really well.

You are escorted by numerous tiny lights, clearly defining the way you must take. Behind you, the lights go out and the forest closes in. You do not look back. The path winds back and forth, first to the left and then the right. It is not long before you have lost your sense of direction. All you can do is to walk the path defined by the lights.

Now the forest is gone, and you are on a plain, looking out across a sea of mist to an island, far off in the morning light. Your escort of lights has gone, but you can now see well enough. Through the mist a boat is coming towards you. Nothing else moves.

There is a figure in the prow of the boat. It is vaguely human in shape, but whether male or female you cannot make out. Even as you step on board the figure remains vague. You speak a greeting, but the gentle motion of the boat sliding through the water is your only reply.

Time has ceased to have any meaning as you pass through the mists over the sea. The shadow in the prow grows, the mists part, and you are

ashore. You have arrived at the Island of the Dragon. You are alone. The barge has gone. There is no way back.

The land before you slopes gradually from the shore, then steepens to form a single hill, standing like a green sentinel above the sea of mist. A path of scaly stones leads off towards the hill, the only way on. You follow the path as it winds slowly round the hill, expecting that it will simply ascend, but it turns back on itself and drops some distance back down the hill before another turn finds you climbing again.

The path goes on and on, climbing, dropping, turning and then climbing again. You begin to tire, and eventually the thought comes to your mind that you will abandon this quest, and try to get back to the safety of your own lands. As you force your increasingly weary legs to go on, fatigue and the desire to turn back become so intolerably strong that you begin to wonder if it is only your aching body that is causing you to think this way.

At last you stop. You stand on the seemingly endless path, perhaps only two hundred yards from the point you first stepped ashore. Going on from here is one of the hardest things you have ever done. The ache in your legs is intense. The sword you carry has become such a burden that you long to leave it behind. And worse, the longing for the safety of your past and the mounting unease about your future is turning your limbs to water.

You go on. The path seems a little easier now, as it climbs more but twists less. Any gratitude you feel is lost in the growing feeling of fear. You can see nothing but the scaly backbone of the hill you are climbing. No birds sing; no sound but the laboured beating of your heart and gasping breaths.

Yet you know that it is coming, whatever it is. The end of your quest is almost here. Your weariness nearly drags you to your knees. Your blood chills in the sudden icy breeze, freezing the sweat on your brow and body. You cannot go on, but you do, dragging the sword after you.

The mists return. You can see nothing. The path ends abruptly at a pit, and you only just manage not to fall in. You send up a grateful little prayer that you were not running, for it is not a pleasant pit. You can see neither the bottom, nor the other side. Forcing yourself to stand, you wait. You do not have to wait long. A red glow rises from the depths of the pit, and your sweat dries as the cold wind loses its power. The temperature continues to rise as the glow in the pit becomes intense. You begin to sweat again. You must run, but where to? You must get away from this accursed place, but you cannot move. Your feet are rooted to the spot.

The ground is vibrating now, and the air is scorching. You can feel the sword in your hand burning your skin. It seems that you will be consumed in this unbearable heat. Your thin armour burns into your skin, and you begin to panic. A voice inside your head tells you to throw away the sword, tear off your armour before it burns you to the bone. The last remnants of your warrior's pride prevent you from dropping your only means of defence.

Instead, you raise the sword over your head as the now-blinding light emerges from the pit. The earth itself crashes down as the Dragon finally emerges from its lair. The pit is gone, and there is nothing but the sword in your hand and the dazzling radiance of the Dragon.

You know you cannot win, yet you must try. With the concentrated effort of all your mind, dedicated to a single cause, you match the mindless power of the beast. As your sword strikes, power and will touch and mingle together. Darkness. . .

The peace of oblivion passes, and you regain your identity. At last you know. You are St Michael, and you are also the Dragon. As you contemplate your new state of being, you find that your body has been consumed in defeating the beast. Yet you are not formless. Men have raised a memorial to you; a stone tower to last forever. On hills all over the land they have raised towers to commemorate your act of overcoming the blind energy of the stars. They do not realize that the contest was only drawn. No-one won. For although Man now sees himself as the master of force, you know the truth.

You can but watch as Man's self-importance and arrogance abuse the power won for him at such cost. In the face of such ignorance, how much longer will the Dragon be prepared to stay down in the pit? Would you be prepared to fight again for the race Man has become?

We are all St Michael, and we are all the Dragon. We are all the race of Mankind. Remember this, as the mists swirl about you, and you return to your own world.

A MICHAELMAS GHOST STORY

This is a legend attached to Canterbury Cathedral in Kent. On the night of 29 September, the ghost of Nan Cook walks in the passage known as the Dark Entry. She is going to her execution, for she had murdered her lover, the abbot, with ground glass. On Michaelmas night, early in the fourteenth century, she was walled up for her crime.

The Entry used to be locked at both ends by the Church authorities, because it was thought that anyone who saw her wraith or whom she breathed on, would die within the year.

A MICHAELMAS HERB

Old country lore states that you should never pick blackberries after Michaelmas Day, for then they belong to the Devil. One story says that the Devil fell from Heaven on this day, straight into a bramble bush. He was so angry that he spat on the bush and cursed any blackberries left on its branches.

I am not sure how true this is, but the only time I picked a blackberry after this magic date it was occupied by a wasp. I spent several days in hospital recovering from my allergic reaction to the sting.

BLACKBERRY KITTENS

Any young animal born on this day was thought to be particularly naughty. Kittens were called blackberry kittens, and if tortoiseshell, were considered very lucky. Cats, of course, are traditionally associated with witches. A witch was supposed to be able to transform herself into a cat nine times during her life. This is the origin of the well-known saying every cat has nine lives.

MICHAELMAS SYMBOLS

Michaelmas falls at the beginning of Libra, the Cardinal Air sign. Libra is ruled by Venus, and governs partnerships, the Seventh House. It is greatly concerned with balance and harmony. Saturn is exalted, which usually means limitations, a warning not to run before you can walk. The Egyptian Goddess ruling Libra is Ma'at, who is the Judge; and it is right that its Tarot card should be Justice, Hebrew Lamed. This card indicates innate ability, again according to Case, 'that which guides and urges the manifestation of the Cosmic power represented by the Fool'. She carries the scales of balance, though her sword is of steel, attributed to Mars, with whom Venus had a clandestine affair.

The colour for Libra is green, the colour attributed to Venus, and the gem stone is emerald.

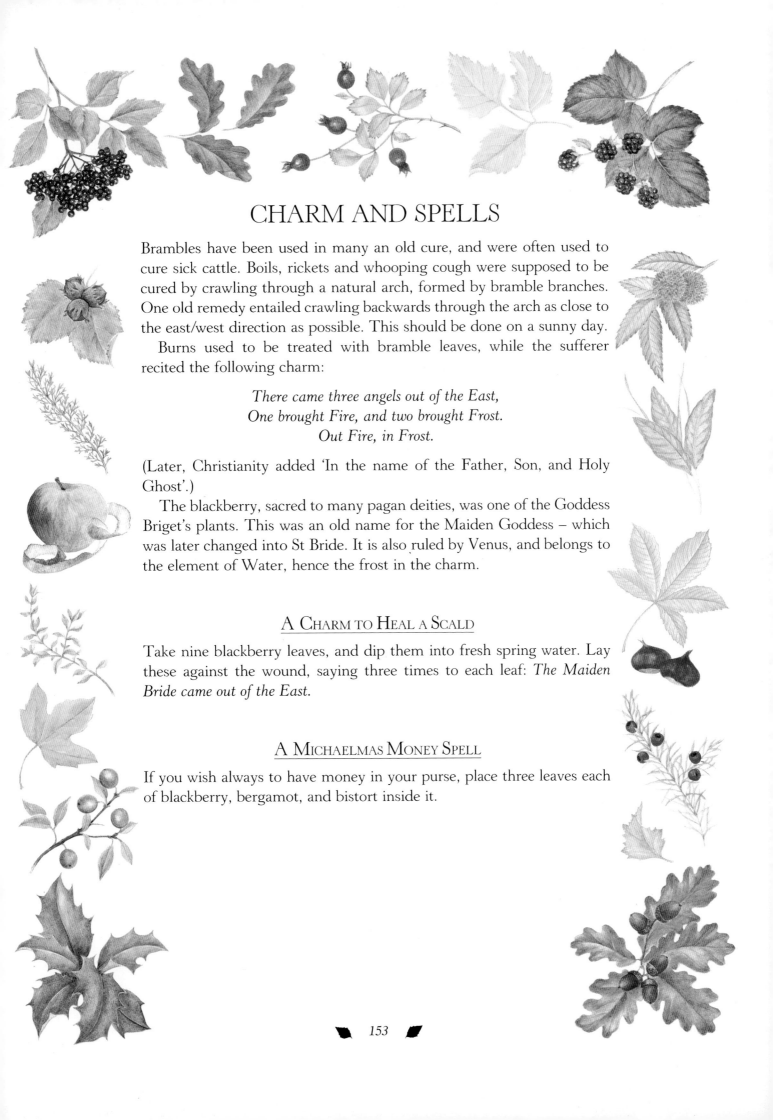

CHARM AND SPELLS

Brambles have been used in many an old cure, and were often used to cure sick cattle. Boils, rickets and whooping cough were supposed to be cured by crawling through a natural arch, formed by bramble branches. One old remedy entailed crawling backwards through the arch as close to the east/west direction as possible. This should be done on a sunny day.

Burns used to be treated with bramble leaves, while the sufferer recited the following charm:

There came three angels out of the East,
One brought Fire, and two brought Frost.
Out Fire, in Frost.

(Later, Christianity added 'In the name of the Father, Son, and Holy Ghost'.)

The blackberry, sacred to many pagan deities, was one of the Goddess Briget's plants. This was an old name for the Maiden Goddess – which was later changed into St Bride. It is also ruled by Venus, and belongs to the element of Water, hence the frost in the charm.

A Charm to Heal a Scald

Take nine blackberry leaves, and dip them into fresh spring water. Lay these against the wound, saying three times to each leaf: *The Maiden Bride came out of the East.*

A Michaelmas Money Spell

If you wish always to have money in your purse, place three leaves each of blackberry, bergamot, and bistort inside it.

FULL CIRCLE

31 OCTOBER

Gather in, gather in, all that has been herein,
Gather in, gather in, so that no trace may be seen,
No trace to mar the sunlit days, or frighten folk
Not of our ways.

Gather in, gather in, all that has been herein.

THE WHEEL HAS TURNED once more, and we have
come round again to Samhaine. This time of year is
one of looking back at what we have done, and
forward to what we are about to do. Here at the
end, we begin the next spiral. We grow with each
season, but if we have not learned, then our
growing will have been in vain.

In the course of a year's work we should find out
a great deal about the world in which we live by
studying the trees, plants, birds and animals of
each season. But most of all we must find out about
ourselves – for if we do not, nothing else matters.

A WITCH'S DIARY

Throughout the year we should have written up our notebooks as we went along. In this way we can look back on the fun, laughter, and sometimes the tears which every year brings. Many of us will have said, 'Well, I'll just make quick notes now, and fill them in in the winter'. But we are not hibernating animals, however much we would like to be. There are always calls upon our time and hospitality, and things get left until we can no longer remember them exactly. Which rite was which? When did we use outdoor sparklers indoors by mistake? Who disturbed a pathworking by scratching her leg? We forget the priestess tripping over the cat, which had somehow managed to creep in when no-one was looking. Or the time someone swore very loudly when he spilled hot candle-wax on his bare foot. Yet, amusing as these incidents are, they should also be noted. They will teach us to be careful with candles, put the cat out more firmly, or buy the right kind of sparklers in future.

Besides the major festivals described here, there are many other rites. These are working rites; for healing, making talismans and potions, because there is a new Moon, or even because it has been a nice day. These, too, are written up together with any dreams or other events which might have a bearing, meditations, reactions and so on. Everything has a purpose, and everything can show us something new.

THE FIRES OF HELL

These days many people fear death. Yet it is only the end of one particular spiral; we believe that it is also the beginning of the next.

For centuries Hell has been portrayed as an accursed place, full of pain and woe, where miserable sinners will pay for their misdeeds in this life. But is this really so? Helle was one of the names of Persephone, when she descended to the Otherworld to become its Queen. She appears on the famous silver cauldron which was recovered from a peat bog in Gundestrup, Denmark. Here she is shown plunging the souls of the departed into its depths.

However, the cauldron is in fact an ancient female symbol. Far from dropping the souls into eternal purgatory, the Goddess is dipping them into the Waters of Inspiration. In this way, she is washing away all the pain, anguish, and anxiety accumulated on this earthly journey. After the souls have been purged, or made pure, they may rest until they are reborn. Cerridwen, a Celtic name for the Goddess, also presided over a Cauldron of Inspiration and Science, which signified rebirth and regeneration.

DEATH AND REBIRTH

Avalon, the Celtic heaven, should not be confused with Annwn, the Otherworld. In Avalon trees bore both flowers and fruit simultaneously, and was a magical place where the soul could rest, and meditate upon all that it had learned in its past life on Earth. Eventually, it would be born again into another loop of the spiral, to continue its education.

Of course, if the soul failed to learn from experience, it would keep returning to the same old place, and the same old problems. This happens throughout life. We keep tripping over the same root until we finally see it is there and do something about it. It may not be pleasant to confront problems, but face them we must – if not in this life, then certainly in the next. By the next life, I mean the next incarnation – not heaven or hell.

I wrote the following verse for a friend whose wife had died. He couldn't face the thought of what lay beyond.

Be not afraid, for the Lady bids you come
Here where the trees are full of blossoms and fair fruit,
Where you are washed of pain, and being numb,
And all the problems of the world are mute.
Here you are purged of all your woes and fears,
And the Hag, who is your Mother, dries your tears.

A FINAL BLESSING

We ask a blessing on the Earth our home,
All who have been here, are here now, and will be in time to come.
We ask the Old Gods to bless us when we come to the end
Of our own particular dance.
So may it be.

ACKNOWLEDGMENTS

The publishers would like to thank the following organizations and individuals for their kind permission to reproduce the photographs in this book:

Frank Lane Picture Agency/David Grewcock 6/Silvestris 17, 51, 62-63, 81/ Ray Bird 18, 54-55, 94, 159/J. Hutchings 22, 44/R. Wilmshurst 31, 41, 45, 47, 120-121/N.A. Elkins 33/Roger Tidman 40, 52, 61, 151/A.R. Hamblin 46, 74-75, 77/J. Watkins 48/Peggy Heard 50, 105, 124/Fritz Polking 66/ Lee Rue 76/M. Nimmo 78, 86-87/Michael Rose 89/Rolf Bender 91/ R.P. Lawrence 97, 136/Martin Withers 123/R. Thompson 125/M.J. Thomas 111, 126, 135, 150/Leo Battan 107/Peter Reynolds 108/Chris Newton 112/ Im Buchenwald 147

Mary Evans Picture Library 30, 32, 67, 93, 110, 127, 139, 140, 152

Colin Molyneux 11, 12-13, 15, 26, 29, 42, 102-103, 106, 118, 145

Neil Holmes/Octopus Group Ltd., 137

Spectrum Colour Library 2, 156

Werner Forman Archive/Statens Historiska Museet, Stockholm 65/ National Museum, Copenhagen 157

Thanks also to Nicki Kemball for the border illustrations.